REVOLUTIONARY
BERLIN

"A guide through Berlin's riveting history that is gripping,
tragic, triumphant and above all, authentic."

Dan Arrows, host of The Iron Dice podcast

"Fascinating and eclectic. This guidebook illuminates hidden
histories with clarity, honesty, wit and irony. Read it and walk it!"

David Rosenberg, author of *Rebel Footprints:*
A Guide to Uncovering London's Radical History

"Inspirational. This collection of walking tours of Red Berlin is
full of wonderful tales from a city which has, despite everything,
remained experimental and revolutionary while others have
become little more than malls or museums, all related with a
deliciously bone-dry Berlinische humor."

Owen Hatherley, author of *Red Metropolis:*
Socialism and the Government of London

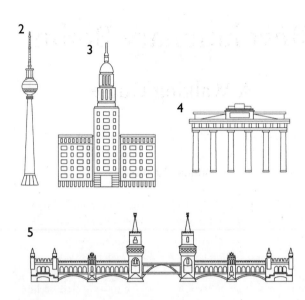

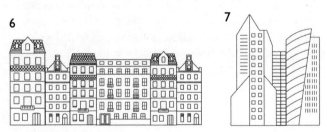

Key:
1. Generic modernist housing project — See Stops 1.11, 2.10, 4.8, 6.1, and 9.5, for example
2. Fernsehturm — See Stop 7.7
3. Stalinallee — See Stop 7.2
4. Brandenburg Gate — See Stop 1.1
5. Oberbaum Bridge — See Stop 9.9
6. Nikolaiviertel — See Introduction
7. Potsdamer Platz — See Stops 2.1 and 6.4

Revolutionary Berlin

A Walking Guide

Nathaniel Flakin

First published 2022 by Pluto Press
New Wing, Somerset House, Strand, London WC2R 1LA

www.plutobooks.com

Copyright © Nathaniel Flakin 2022

Maps by Elemer

The right of Nathaniel Flakin to be identified as the author of this work has
been asserted in accordance with the Copyright, Designs and Patents Act
1988.

Every effort has been made to trace copyright holders and to obtain their
permission for the use of copyright material in this book. The publisher
apologises for any errors or omissions in this respect and would be grateful
if notified of any corrections that should be incorporated in future reprints or
editions.

British Library Cataloguing in Publication Data
A catalogue record for this book is available from the British Library

ISBN 978 0 7453 4642 7   Hardback
ISBN 978 0 7453 4641 0   Paperback
ISBN 978 0 7453 4645 8   PDF
ISBN 978 0 7453 4643 4   EPUB

This book is printed on paper suitable for recycling and made from fully
managed and sustained forest sources. Logging, pulping and manufacturing
processes are expected to conform to the environmental standards of the
country of origin.

Typeset by Stanford DTP Services, Northampton, England

Simultaneously printed in the United Kingdom and United States of America

Dedicated to Peter Wolter (1947–2018), my favorite Stalinist spy, and Wolfgang Wippermann (1945–2021), my favorite old social democrat.*

* Peter Wolter was a journalist who headed Reuters's London bureau — and also a lifelong agent of the Ministry of State Security under the code name "Pirol." He was my first boss when I started working in journalism (More on him at Stop 7.8). Wolfgang Wippermann was a history professor who worked at the Free University Berlin — and also a lifelong member of the Social Democratic Party. Without him, it's hard to picture how I would have gotten a history degree. More on him in my obituary: "Goodbye to Berlin's last left-wing historian," *Exberliner* (online), January 20, 2021.

Only violence can help where violence rules.
Only people can help where there are people.
— Bertolt Brecht, *Saint Joan of the Stockyards*

CONTENTS

ACKNOWLEDGEMENTS

I would like to thank all the people who have joined my walking tours since 2009. This has been more fun for me than for you — but it seems like most of you had an OK time as well.

I would like to thank Bruce Kayton, who wrote a wonderful book called *Radical Walking Tours in New York City*. When I lived in Brooklyn, I visited just about every place he described, and even developed my own walking tours on that basis. Seeing where John Reed or Leon Trotsky used to hang out in Manhattan gave me a deep sense of connection to an otherwise alienating island.

I would like to thank so many historians who have dug into Berlin's radical history. But special mention goes to Wolfgang Wippermann, who passed away in early 2020. Not only did he guide me to a degree in history — on my first day in college, he took a group of students on a critical walking tour through the Free University of Berlin. Everything here is thanks to his example of how to be a merrily belligerent left-wing historian. Thanks also go to Ralf Hoffrogge, who has been an advisor and role model as a lefty historian in the twenty-first century — he even allowed me to steal the idea for a walking tour on the November Revolution.

Thanks to everyone who read the manuscript: Bethany, David, Kate, Kathrin, Marcel, Neal, Nico, Sam, Stefan, and Yossi.

Finally, thanks to David Castle and all the people at Pluto Press for steering this project to publication. Without a fairly

ACKNOWLEDGEMENTS

tight word limit and a very tight deadline, I never would have been able to finish this.

ABBREVIATIONS AND GERMAN WORDS

AL   Alternative Liste — Alternative List (West Berlin)
APO   Außerparlamentarische Opposition — Extra
          Parliamentary Opposition
ASB   Arbeiter-Samariter-Bund — Workers Samaritan
          League
AStA   Allgemeiner Studentenausschuss (today:
          Studierenden) — General Students' Committee
CDU   Christlich Demokratische Union — Christian
          Democratic Union
CYI   Communist Youth International
DGB   Deutscher Gewerkschaftsbund — German Trade
          Union Confederation
FDJ   Freie Deutsche Jugend — Free German Youth
FRG   Bundesrepublik Deutschland — Federal Republic of
          Germany
GDR   Deutsche Demokratische Republik — German
          Democratic Republic
GKSD   Garde-Kavallerie-Schützen-Division — Guards
          Cavalry Rifle Division
HAW   Homosexuelle Aktion Westberlin — Homosexual
          Action West Berlin
HIB   Homosexuelle Interessengemeinschaft Berlin —
          Homosexual Interest Group Berlin (East)
ISD   Initiative Schwarzer Menschen in Deutschland —
          Initiative of Black People in Germany

ABBREVIATIONS AND GERMAN WORDS

KPD   Kommunistische Partei Deutschlands — Communist
          Party of Germany

RAF   Rote Armee Fraktion — Red Army Faction

SA   Sturmabteilung — Storm Detachment (Nazi
          paramilitary organization)

S-Bahn   Stadtbahn — city railway (urban trains)

S-Bhf   S-Bahnhof — S-Bahn station

SDKPiL   Socjaldemokracja Królestwa Polskiego i Litwy —
          Social Democracy of the Kingdom of Poland and
          Lithuania

SDS   Sozialistischer Deutscher Studentenbund — Socialist
          German Student League, 1946–70 (Also: Students for
          a Democratic Society, U.S., 1960–74)

SED   Sozialistische Einheitspartei — Socialist Unity Party

SPD   Sozialdemokratische Partei Deutschlands — Social
          Democratic Party of Germany (during the war also
          known as the Majority SPD or MSPD)

Stasi   Ministerium für Staatssicherheit — Ministry of State
          Security (East Germany)

SWAPO   South West Africa People's Organization (Namibia)

VLO   Vereinigte Linke Opposition der KPD (Bolschewiki-
          Leninisten) — United Left Opposition of the KPD
          (Bolshevik-Leninists)

U-Bahn   Undergrundbahn — underground railway (subway)

U-Bhf   U-Bahnhof — U-Bahn station

USPD   Unabhängige Sozialdemokratische Partei
          Deutschlands — Independent Social Democratic
          Party of Germany

* * *

Bundestag — West German parliament (1949–present)

Gründerzeit ("founders' time") — Period of rapid economic expansion after the foundation of the German Empire in 1871, lasting until roughly 1900

Kiez — Berlin slang for neighborhood

Plattenbau — Prefabricated concrete apartment blocks, especially common in East Germany

Reichstag — German parliament / parliament building (1871-present)

Ring / Ringbahn — Ring train / the circle line of the S-Bahn, the unofficial boundary between the inner and the outer city

Stolperstein (literally: stumbling stone) — Commemorative brass cobblestone placed in front of the homes of people who were deported, killed, or forced to flee under the Nazis

INTRODUCTION

Berlin is such a young city. The first record of a town here is from 1237 — not even 800 years ago. When Berlin was just a collection of huts along the river Spree, Parisians had been constructing the Notre Dame Cathedral for several generations. The German capital only reached 1 million inhabitants by 1880. London had cracked that record almost a century earlier. Rome was that size in the second century.

Does Berlin even have a history? The past does tend to fade away when the drugs kick in at a dark club. It can feel like the city's architectural tumult — Stalinist baroque, decaying industry, and shiny office towers — fell straight from the sky.

So much of the city was razed to the ground that its history can take on a postmodern, Disneyland-like feeling. Look closely at the oldest district, the Nikolaiviertel, for example — most of it was actually built in 1987 in the East German prefab concrete style.

Berlin's history, buried under many layers of ruins, is short but intense. In the last 150 years, the city has passed through at least half a dozen different political regimes. As the travel writer Jan Morris put it, Berlin bears the "stigmata of Prussian militarism, Weimar decadence, Nazi evil, Stalinist oppression and tawdry capitalist excess." Each has left its marks on both the architecture and the mentality. Berlin ran the gauntlet through the Age of Extremes — it's daunting to summarize everything in one slim volume.

To name an example: Buckingham Palace has been home to the same criminal dynasty for two centuries. One could write plenty about them, but it would be a more or less contiguous story.

Berlin's City Palace, in contrast, was once home to the Hohen-zollern dynasty. It was a backdrop for the beginning of World War I in 1914. Four years later, it was a key site for a workers' rev-olution — a few weeks before being bombarded by proto-fascist paramilitaries. Then it was bombed in World War II, and the rubble was carted away in 1950 (with different parts ending up all over the city). In 1976, a new palace was put in its place: East Germany's Palace of the Republic. That bronze-colored hulk was torn down in 2006 to symbolize the triumph of capitalism. Now, the old City Palace has been rebuilt from scratch, and it houses an ethnological museum full of stolen colonial artifacts. (See Stop 2.2) A lot to cover!

This book is going to be just as chaotic as Berlin's history. I will use the same impatient and aggrieved tone that has always characterized Berliners. The closest thing we have to a local hymn is called "Berlin stinkt!" (Berlin stinks), a song in which the chanson punk band The Incredible Herrengedeck sums up the city's missed potential: "Where have the Golden Twenties gone? Beer was cheap and communism was a real possibility!" Berliners have this sense of bitter, nostalgic disappointment pre-cisely because utopia has always been visible as a glow just over the horizon. This contradiction between the bright future and the gray present has erupted again and again, generation after gener-ation, in the form of rebellions and even revolutions.

Most of the revolts that will be covered in this book were unsuccessful. But that is nothing new. Karl Marx, who lived in the city briefly in the late 1830s and early 1840s, used to joke that the Germans shared all the counterrevolutions of other peoples but none of the revolutions. Rosa Luxemburg, the star of this book, explained that defeats are inevitable, and even necessary:

revolution is the only form of 'war' ... in which the ultimate victory can be prepared only by a series of 'defeats.' ... Today, as we advance into the final battle of the proletarian class war, we stand on the foundation of those very defeats; and we cannot do without *any* of them, because each one contributes to our strength and understanding. ... these unavoidable defeats pile up guarantee upon guarantee of the future final victory.

This book will tell the stories of earlier generations who fought, and more often than not lost. Studying their experiences will prepare the ground for new revolutions. We are going to cover a lot of stuff that might seem depressing — but the comrades who held out on the different barricades throughout the ages would surely want to be remembered as being full of hope for the future.

How to read this book

So how to distill hundreds of history books and millions of stories into just nine self-guided tours? I am going to rely on my personal obsessions. Why is there a chapter on Red Neukölln and none on Red Wedding, for example? Because I live in the former and the latter is really far away. This is not intended to be a comprehensive history — rather, this book will hopefully entertain, and eventually inspire people to write their own, better books. I am also hoping to leave my own mark on the city — I got a commemorative brass cobblestone (Stolperstein) placed for the metalworker and Trotskyist leader Anton Grylewicz in June 2021, and another Stolperstein for KPD chairwoman Ruth Fischer should be placed in February 2022. Someday I hope to get a historical plaque put up for the "man behind Rosa Luxemburg," Leo Jogiches. (See Stops 4.5, 4.6, and 4.9)

Writing a guidebook, I am confronted with the same difficulty faced by every socialist historian: The people who risk the most to join a protest, and who therefore have the greatest impact on history, are the least likely to commit their experiences to writing. The participation of common people is precisely what defines a revolution. It is not about Rosa Luxemburg giving a speech — Luxemburg gave speeches just about every day of her life. A revolution is when bus drivers, nurses, and drag queens start doing things that they could have never imagined doing. So these walks will try, as best as possible, to recount the histories of these anonymous masses. But I would like to apologize to all the Berlin rebels that such a work of history inevitably overlooks.

This book is organized into nine walks. The first six of them are real walking tours that I developed over the last ten years — they have been endlessly revised and perfected with live audiences. The last three are new for this book — they were written down during a pandemic that made it impossible to show groups of strangers around the city.

Each number on a map corresponds to a stop in the same chapter. So in Chapter 2, the number 7 on the map on page 39 refers to Stop 2.7 on page 52.

This book is dedicated to generations of Berliners who saw the outlines of a future beyond capitalism and decided to make sacrifices and take risks to make it a reality.

Berlin really does stink. But the hope for a better tomorrow is still present, right beneath the cobblestones.

To view the locations on Google Maps please go to:
https://revolutionaryberlin.wordpress.com/map/

Martin Dibobe, Berlin's first Black subway driver, at U-Bhf Schlesisches Tor in 1902. See Stop 1.3. Photographer unknown. Courtesy of BVG-Archiv.

1

(Anti)Colonialism

1.1. Brandenburg Gate
Brandenburger Tor, Pariser Platz

We are going to start our first tour at Brandenburg Gate — not just because every Berlin tour starts here, but because it is a good place to talk about German history. Berlin is not well-known as a colonial metropolis. Germany entered the "great game" late, but it entered with a vengeance. Starting in the 1880s, the German Empire conquered vast swaths of Africa, as well as territories in Asia and the Pacific

Germany lost its "place in the sun" in World War I and failed to reclaim it in World War II. Nonetheless, in just a few decades of German colonialism, hundreds of thousands of people were massacred. This included the first German genocide.

* * *

Despite all pretensions to the contrary, Deutschland is a young nation-state — the United States of America was almost 100 years old before the first united German state was founded. Therefore, the history of German colonialism is far older than the country itself.

Before there was Germany, Berlin was part of Prussia; and before that, it belonged to the Margraviate of Brandenburg. It

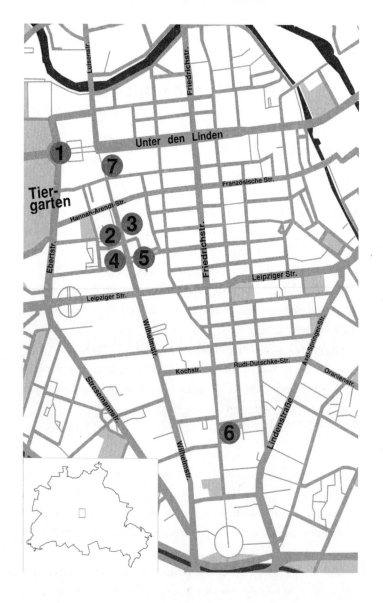

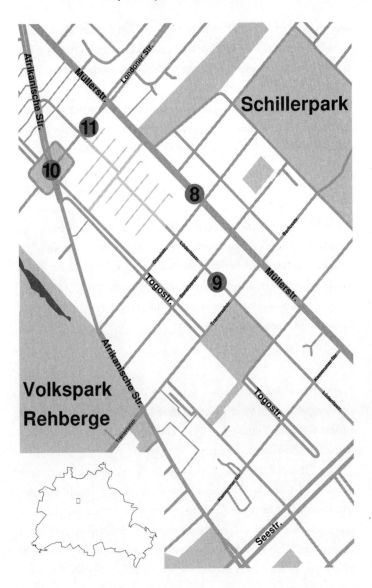

was an aristocrat from Brandenburg who led the first "German" expedition to Africa. On January 1, 1683, Friedrich Otto von der Groeben established a fort on the Gold Coast (today Ghana). He christened it Groß Friedrichsburg.

Over the next 35 years, this German fort was a nexus for the European slave trade. Up to 30,000 Africans were enslaved and imprisoned here, before being sold to sugar plantations in the Caribbean.

In 1717, the new king in Prussia, Friedrich Wilhelm I, gave up on colonialism in order to focus on building a continental army. He sold Groß Friedrichsburg and a few more holdings to the Dutch West India Company for "7,200 ducats and 12 moors."

Von der Groeben had a street named after him in Berlin in 1895, when German colonial fever was at its peak. 115 years later, Groebenufer was the first colonial street name in the city to be changed. (See Stop 9.9)

* * *

German colonialism died down for almost 200 years. It only reemerged after Prussia's victory over France and the foundation of the German Empire in 1871. The new German imperialism turned its gaze back to Africa.

The "Iron Chancellor" Otto von Bismarck is best known for uniting 26 Central European mini-states into a single empire. But he actually conquered more territory in Africa. By the time Germany began its colonial endeavors, Africa had largely been carved up. The French had established a colony in Algeria in 1830 and went on to rule most of West Africa. The British were attempting to build a colony stretching from "the Cape to Cairo," so from the south to the north of the continent. German colonialists had to find niches left over by earlier colonial powers. Within 15 years, they claimed four colonies: Togoland, now Togo; Cameroon; German South West Africa, which is today Namibia; and German East Africa, which now includes parts of Tanzania, Rwanda, and Burundi.

1.2. Reich Chancellery
Wilhelmstraße 92 (formerly 77)

Wilhelmstraße is not much of a street today: South of Unter den Linden, it is lined with prefabricated concrete apartment buildings in the style of the German Democratic Republic. When we turn the corner at the Hotel Adlon to enter Wilhelmstraße, we pass through traffic barriers that have permanently closed this section of the street to cars. This is to protect the British Embassy, which is clearly a new building (opened in 2000). But the representatives of the United Kingdom have been residing at this location since 1884.

Wilhelmstraße was once the main axis of Prussian and imperial Berlin. Ministers, ambassadors, aristocrats, and capitalists had their palaces along this street. Historical panels on the sidewalk explain the long history of almost every address. Two blocks south of the British embassy, at Wilhelmstraße 92, we see nothing but more brown apartment blocks. It requires some imagination to picture an imposing palace behind iron gates and a manicured garden.

This was the seat of power in the German Empire: The Reich Chancellery of Otto von Bismarck. Only after he had consolidated his new empire in central Europe did Bismarck turn to colonial competition. His policy for Africa can best be summed up with a German idiom: If two people fight, then a third is happy. So while the British and French were wrangling to be the dominant power in Africa, the Germans presented themselves as mediators. Bismarck invited representatives from 14 colonial powers to his palace in November 1884. (Or to be more precise: powers with colonial pretensions — the United States, for example, had not yet acquired any overseas colonies.)

The 14 diplomats had one main question to solve: While the African coasts had largely been divided up, who would control the massive Congo Basin, an area larger than Western Europe?

This three-month meeting thus became known as the Kongokonferenz (or more commonly in English: the Berlin Conference). Fourteen men sitting around a table in Wilhelmstraße, without a single African present, drew borders across Africa — borders that, with a few modifications, remain to this day. The French wanted to prevent the British from claiming the Congo, just as the British wanted to block the French; both didn't want to see the rising German Empire seize such vast riches.

The Congo ultimately went to Belgium. But not to the state of Belgium, which would have implied some measure of control for the Belgian parliament — the colony instead became the personal property of King Leopold II. The new Belgian colonial administration exploited the peoples of the Congo ruthlessly. In two decades, up to 10 million Africans were massacred — among the largest genocides in history. Thankfully, today statues of Leopold II are finally being torn down.

(ANTI)COLONIALISM

At the end of the Congo Conference, just a handful of African states remained independent. Ethiopia, then known as Abyssinia, was the only African state that was never subjugated. Liberia was founded by former slaves from the United States and stood under Washington's tutelage. Morocco held out at this time, but was later divided between France and Spain. Kingdoms in what is today Libya and also on the Horn of Africa remained independent as well, but were conquered by Italian imperialism in the early twentieth century.

In 2004, a historical plaque was installed on the sidewalk to mark the 120th anniversary of the Berlin Conference.

1.3. Imperial Colonial Office
roughly Wilhelmstraße 51 (formerly 62)

Opposite the old Reich Chancellery, and a bit to the north, we see a primary school made of bricks and concrete. Visualizing what used to be here again requires some imagination. A four-story government building once housed the Imperial Colonial Office, founded in 1907 under the second Kaiser Wilhelm as a central administration for the Empire's far-flung possessions. This included the military command of the so-called Schutztruppen, the cynically named "protective troops."

The office became superfluous after Germany lost its colonies with the Treaty of Versailles in 1919, and it was dissolved in 1920. Yet the government of the Weimar Republic never fully accepted the loss — the slogan "we demand a place in the sun" (first spoken by Reich Chancellor Bernhard von Bülow in 1897) remained popular throughout the 1920s. A special section of the Foreign Office for colonial affairs was created in 1925.

When power was handed over to the Nazis in 1933, they had ambitious plans for conquests in the East, but also in Africa. They created a Colonial-Political Office where hundreds of state officials worked out regulations for native peoples in the future Nazi-ruled Africa. Of course, while the Nazis' Afrika Korps made some initial conquests in North Africa, they were never able to establish a colony. As a result, one historian has called this office "the world's most sophisticated colonial administration without any actual colonies." A very German way to do things!

Since 2019, the Berlin government has commemorated this location with a plaque next to the Ikarus youth center. It is dedicated to Martin Dibobe, a famous Black Berliner from before World War I. He had come to Berlin to serve as an artifact at the German Colonial Exposition of 1896 (See Stop 1.8) and later became a U-Bahn driver. In 1919, Dibobe sent a petition to the National Assembly in Weimar, signed by 17 African men living in Germany. They expressed loyalty to Germany — but also included 32 grievances and demands for "equality and autonomy." The German government published the passages in support of German colonial rule and censored the rest. Dibobe tried to return to Cameroon in 1922 and all traces of him disappeared.

1.4. New Reich Chancellery
roughly Wilhelmstraße 94

One block south of the old Reich Chancellery, opposite an entrance to the decadent Mall of Berlin and in front of a Chinese restaurant, we can stand at the spot of perhaps the most infamous building in world history: This long, narrow block was filled with Hitler's megalomaniacal New Reich Chancellery, designed by Albert Speer and opened in 1939. The bunker where Hitler shot himself in 1945 was located underneath.

Hitler could go onto a balcony to speak to crowds gathered on Wilhelmplatz opposite. Looking for this Wilhelm Square in Berlin's modern geography is quite a challenge. Google Maps points us to the traffic island where stairs lead down to the subway. Could many Hitler fans have gathered there? A very old sign informs us this is not Wilhelmplatz but rather Ziethenplatz.

The solution to this mystery is that Wilhelmplatz, which once spanned two city blocks, was eaten up by post-war urban development. The north side was filled with East German apartments in the 1980s. The south side made way for the embassy of the Czechoslovak Socialist Republic, which was completed in 1978. (And while this doesn't have anything to do with this tour, let me say that this ultramodernist spaceship is quite an amazing building! Behind it, the massive grey embassy of the Democratic People's Republic of Korea remains in service but stands largely empty. For many years, the North Koreans rented out their embassy to a hostel, but that had to close due to sanctions.)

At the end of the war, Hitler's chancellery was destroyed but the square remained. At first, all four Allied Powers agreed to rid German city maps of references to Nazis and to the former ruling house, the Hohenzollern dynasty. But the cooperation was short-lived: While all the Hitler Streets were renamed, soon the Western powers decided they did not mind the Prussian kings after all. Thus, only East Berlin got rid of countless street names referring to Wilhelm, Friedrich, Friedrich Wilhelm, and all the other repetitively christened German monarchs.

Wilhelmplatz was renamed Ernst-Thälmann-Platz in 1949, after the leader of the Communist Party of Germany from 1925 until his arrest by the Nazis in 1933. Wilhelmstraße became Otto-Grotewohl-Straße in 1964. That largely forgotten social democratic bureaucrat became, for arcane reasons of Stalinist diplomacy, the first prime minister of the German Democratic Republic.

Today, when activists demand that colonial street names be changed, politicians often claim that this is simply impossible. Older residents have business cards and stationery — you can't just ask them to get such things reprinted! But it turns out, no, it is actually very easy to change street names — they just need to be named after communists. Wilhelmplatz and Wilhelmstraße got their old names back in 1992 and 1993.

1.5. M-Straße
Anton-Wilhelm-Amo-Straße — former Mohrenstraße

For decades, this was the most offensive street name in Berlin. I am going to write it down once, for reference: Mohrenstraße (Moor Street). But many people prefer to say M-Straße, and that is what I will use here.

The street name is old enough that it's hard to say where it originated. The most common theory goes back to the sale of Groß Friedrichsburg at the beginning of the eighteenth century — the payment to the king in Prussia included "12 moors." (See Stop 1.1) And while the Prussian state had plenty of forms of oppression, it did not enslave Black people.

The aristocratic fashion was to keep "court Moors" like animals in a menagerie. These 12 Africans were drafted into the Prussian army to serve as musicians. Some of them married into noble houses and got titles. Their barracks were probably around here somewhere — leading to the name "Moor Street." (This is just one of several possible explanations.)

Is the German word "Mohr" offensive? The short answer is: yes. It is not a common racist epithet in German today. Similar to "moor" in English, it mostly comes up in historical contexts. But this antiquated use is accompanied by repulsive caricatures of Black people. Just imagine the logo of the "Three Moors" hotel (which was only changed in 2020!). German society has been slow to drop such terms. Even in the 2000s, it was not uncommon to hear chocolate-covered marshmallows referred to with the n-word.

People have been demanding that the street be renamed for decades. In early 2009, for example, a giant pink rabbit added two dots to all the street signs. In German, two dots are enough to change a racist term (Mohren) to "carrots" (Möhren). Carrots Street — probably not a serious suggestion, but a practical display of how imminently *easy* a change would be. People who work at a Humboldt University building on this street already write their address as Möhrenstraße and still receive mail.

Conservatives say: You can't change such an old, traditional name! But while the street name is in fact ancient, what about the U-Bahn station? It opened in 1908, but it was originally called U-Bhf Kaiserhof — named after Berlin's swankiest hotel on the north side of Wilhelmplatz. In the 1950s, it was rechristened U-Bhf Ernst-Thälmann-Platz. It kept this name for 35 years, until East Berlin opened an Ernst-Thälmann-Park with an accompanying S-Bahn station in 1986. They decided having two stations with Thälmann would be confusing — especially because the "Platz" in the former name had effectively disappeared. So this became U-Bhf Otto-Grotewohl-Straße. The current name, M-Straße, has only been there since 1991. In other words, this "old, traditional" name is younger than me!

Protests have taken place on the square every year. Activists made numerous proposals for alternative names, such as Nelson-Mandela-Straße or Audre-Lorde-Straße. But year after year, the district council refused to even hold a hearing. A big newspaper wrote that renaming the street would mean "ignoring history." That is a dumb argument, but particularly so in Germany: Should we have kept all of the Hitler Streets to commemorate the Holocaust?

It took militant protests around the world to get things moving. In June 2020, at the height of the Black Lives Matter movement, the Berlin public transport company BVG announced they were renaming the station: Glinkastraße, after the street on the other side of the station. But this idea was also criticized, as the work of the nineteenth century Russian composer Mikhail Glinka contains antisemitic stereotypes.

Then, on August 20, 2020, the district council held a surprise vote. Without any kind of announcement or public participation, they decided the street should be named after Anton Wilhelm Amo. This is a figure who might be able to satisfy conservatives who want to preserve references to Berlin's distant past: Amo was a Black philosopher from the eighteenth century who spent his adult life in Prussia. The Anton-Wilhelm-Amo-Straße was supposed to be inaugurated on October 1, 2021, but this has not yet happened and it's not clear when it will be done.

For ten years, I gave tours about racist street names. In that time, not a single one changed. But now, just as I am writing this book, old names are falling like dominos. The people we have to thank for this are the activists who tore down offensive statues and set fire to police stations around the world in 2020.

1.6. League for the Defense of the Negro Race
former Friedrichstraße 24 — Besselpark

The southern end of Friedrichstraße lacks the neoliberal pretension of the tourist-filled promenade further north. This area was once pressed against the wall, and West Berlin filled it with social housing. Only recently have fancier establishments popped up — none fancier than the metal-clad new headquarters of the *taz* newspaper. The *taz* began as an alternative daily in 1978, but now represents the "green" wing of German imperialism. (See stop 6.8) Besselark is an unremarkable grass square next door.

In the 1920s, a building at Friedrichstraße 24 served as the international headquarters of the League Against Imperialism. In September 1929, 30 Black Berliners, mostly from the former German colony in Cameroon, gathered here to found a German section of the League for the Defense of the Negro Race. The most famous of them was the Afro-German actor Louis Brody who performed in dozens of films. They presented a theatrical revue and even planned to open a Black Theater. But lacking financial resources, the league had to dissolve in 1932. Brody, despite his communist connections, remained successful under the Nazis, as they needed Black actors for their colonialist propaganda films. He had an important role in the 1941 film *Carl Peters*, for example. (See Stop 1.11)

Both these leagues were run by the Communist International, uniting communists and non-communists to campaign for the independence of the colonies. The League Against Imperialism was founded at a conference in Brussels in 1927 that brought together anti-colonial leaders with European leftists and intellectuals: Jawaharlal Nehru rubbed elbows with Albert Einstein.

The driving force behind these fronts was Willi Münzenberg. (See Stop 4.8) Münzenberg ran a communist media empire in Weimar Germany that could compete with the biggest capitalist concerns, and was thus known as "the red millionaire." Münzenberg's headquarters were at the Neuer Deutscher Verlag (New German Publishing House) at Wilhelmstraße 48, which is today a parking lot opposite the Finance Ministry. That is where the *Arbeiter-Illustrierte Zeitung* (Workers Illustrated Magazine) was published, including photographic reports from Soviet Russia and artwork by John Heartfield.

While the African diaspora in Berlin in the 1920s consisted of just 5,000 people or so, this was not the worst place for anti-colonial activists. German police might not even object to people organizing for the independence of French or British colonies. The most famous anti-colonial activist in Germany was George Padmore. He was born in Trinidad as Malcolm Ivan Meredith Nurse, and moved to Harlem to study medicine, where he joined the Communist Party. Padmore went to Moscow in 1929 and was one of the chief organizers of an international conference of Black communists in Hamburg in 1930. They set up an International Trade Union Committee for Negro Workers as part of the Communist International. Their newspaper, *The Negro Worker*, was published in Hamburg — thanks to the harbor, it could easily be distributed across Africa or the Americas.

Padmore was expelled from the Comintern in 1934. This was the time that Stalin began seeking alliances with "democratic" imperialist powers, and thus abandoning anti-colonial agitation. Padmore worked together with C.L.R. James in London and went on to become a leading thinker of pan-Africanism. At the end of his life, he served as an advisor of the first president of independent Ghana, Kwame Nkrumah. His journey passed through Germany.

1.7. Ministry of People's Education
former Ministerium für Volksbildung —
Matthias-Erzberger-Haus — Unter den Linden 71

Opposite the British Embassy, Wilhelmstraße is filled with a two-part building. The older, southern part was built in 1903, as an annex to the Prussian Cultural Ministry on Unter den Linden. The ministry did not survive the war, but the annex did. In 1949, the German Democratic Republic (GDR) put their Ministry of People's Education in the back building. In 1965, they constructed a new front building. This double building now houses offices of the German Bundestag.

What does all this have to do with colonialism? The GDR's longest-serving Minister of People's Education, from 1963 to 1989, was Margot Honecker. After the collapse of East Germany, she went into exile in Santiago de Chile. It is fair to say that she was not a particularly popular figure on the international diplomatic circuit. But in 2005, Margot Honecker was invited to Namibia, where she took part in the official celebrations of the 15th anniversary of the country's independence, as a guest of honor seated in the front row.

This was in recognition of the support that East Germany gave to SWAPO, the South West Africa People's Organization, starting in the 1970s. The GDR sent food and clothing, but also weapons and vehicles to the Namibian independence movement. Injured fighters were brought to East Berlin for treatment, and 400 orphaned children came to live here. East German military and secret service personnel provided training to SWAPO cadres — it seems German soldiers were secretly active in Namibia itself, but it is hard to know for sure through the fog of Cold War propaganda.

Throughout the 1980s, West Germany was supporting the Apartheid regime in South Africa, which ruled over Namibia as well. It pains me to say positive things about the GDR. As a critical communist, I know that people like me were locked up and deported. There were also different forms of anti-Black racism in the country. But East Berlin's support for Namibian independence is an example of concrete anti-colonialism — real atonement for the crimes committed by German imperialism.

1.8. African Quarter
U-Bhf Rehberge, south entrance

Leaving Wilhelmstraße and the district of Mitte, we can get on the subway line U6 heading north under Friedrichstraße. After 14 minutes, getting out at U-Bhf Rehberge in Wedding, we find ourselves in the middle of Berlin's African Quarter. And this is a bit strange: When you enter Chinatown in Manhattan, you will be surrounded by Chinese culture. But not much in the African Quarter appears African. The history of this kiez is only very indirectly connected to African people.

The African Quarter has 21 streets and one square with names relating to Africa. 18 of these are innocuous: There is a Togostraße, a Kongostraße, a Sansibarstraße, and so on. In 1958, a Ghanastraße was created right after the Gold Coast became independent under a new name. Three streets are named after colonial mass murderers — we will look at them in a moment.

The history of this neighborhood actually starts across the city, in Treptower Park. In 1896, the first German Colonial Exhibition took place there — a sort of world fair to showcase Germany's overseas possessions. The organizers had brought 103 people from the colonies. The highlight was a so-called "Negro village" displaying people next to mud huts with straw roofs. Over the summer, up to 2 million people visited the grounds next to Trepwtow's Karpfenteich (carp pond). The problem: The Africans who had made the voyage belonged to local elites, including Friedrick Maharero the son of the chief of the Herero people. They presented themselves wearing European suits and carrying rifles. One colonialist doubted that all Herero would "make such a thoroughly distinguished impression and accomplish such gentleman-like stature."

Carl Hagenbeck, a North German entrepreneur who founded the zoo in Hamburg (which still bears his name), had an idea. It is a dirty secret of German zoos that until the 1950s, they would display not just animals but also human beings — people who were referred to as "bush men" or "pygmies." After the success of the Treptow exhibition, Hagenbeck began planning a permanent "human zoo," to be located in Rehberge park. The streets built around it all got names relating to Africa. Construction of the zoo, however, was interrupted by World War I. And by the time the war was over, Germany had no more colonial subjects to display like animals. The street names remained.

1.9. Adolf Lüderitz
Lüderitzstraße

Lüderitz is not just the name of this multicultural, proletarian street in Wedding. Lüderitz is also the name of a small city in southern Namibia. Both are named after Adolf Lüderitz, a North German merchant who founded the colony in South West Africa.

Shark Island is a peninsula jutting out into Lüderitz Bay. This "half-island" was the site of Germany's first concentration camp. It was built in 1904 — 35 years before the beginning of the Holocaust — to put down an anti-colonial uprising.

Starting in 1904, the Herero and Nama peoples of Namibia rose up against their German "protectors." They were pejoratively referred to as "Hottentots." This is how the reclusive postmodern author Thomas Pynchon — you might have seen him with a paper bag over his head on The Simpsons — described the German response in his novel V:

[Hanging] had been a popular form of killing during the Great Rebellion of 1904–7, when the Hereros and Hottentots, who usually fought one another, staged a simultaneous but

uncoordinated rising against an incompetent German administration. General Lothar von Trotha ... was brought in to
deal with the Hereros. In August 1904, von Trotha issued
his 'Vernichtungs-Befehl' [Extermination Order], whereby
German forces were ordered to exterminate systematically
every Herero man, woman and child they could find. He
was about 80 percent successful. Out of the estimated 80,000
Hereros living in the territory in 1904, an official German
census taken seven years later set the Herero population at
only 15,130, this being a decrease of 64,870 ... von Trotha ...
is reckoned to have done away with about 60,000 people. This
is only 1 percent of six million, but still pretty good.

In total, about 80% of the Herero and 50% of the Nama were
eliminated. The German troops did not just rely on hanging:
They also drove people out into the desert to die of thirst, while
survivors were worked to death in concentration camps.

Pynchon's chilling words draw the connection to the next,
much larger German genocide — and it is not just postmodern
novelists who recognize the continuities. Hitler's plans to acquire
"living space" for the Germans were taken straight from colonial
ideology. There was also a process of what we could call "institutional learning." Von Trotha's Extermination Order was
published by competing imperialist powers to present Germany
as being unusually brutal. This provided lessons for the next
genocide, and the Nazis consistently avoided putting their plans
for a "Final Solution" in writing.

The German government, however, is reluctant to use the
G-word. They recognize genocides in Armenia or in Kosovo,

but not in Namibia. The legal arguments are absurd — perhaps genocide wasn't explicitly prohibited by law in 1904? In 2021, the German government announced it had reached an agreement with the Namibian government that would recognize a genocide — but only in a moral, and not in a legal sense. Germany's foreign minister said this distinction was important to oppose demands for reparations. Descendants of the Herero and Nama peoples rejected the deal as a "PR coup."

1.10. *Gustav Nachtigal*
Nachtigalplatz

Walking north from Lüderitzstraße, we will cross one of Berlin's small "garden colonies." Visitors from the Third World sometimes wonder if these are massive shanty towns. They are in fact garden parcels for people who live in apartments. Of course, there are cases of people living in the unheated shacks, but that is not their intended purpose.

This one, sitting on Togostraße, used to be called the "Permanent Colony Togo." After several years of anti-colonial tours going through the kiez, the name was changed to the "Small Garden Association Togo." Progress! In fact, the only progress so far in this neighborhood. It also appears that right-wing flags from the German Empire or the Confederacy are also slowly disappearing from the plots.

This will take us to Nachtigalplatz — named after Gustav Nachtigal, who founded the German colonies in Cameroon and Togo. The Wikipedia entry for Nachtigal describes him as an "explorer" — and that term, in that period, should make our hair stand on end. Nachtigal travelled across the Sahara and was named Bismarck's special commissioner for West Africa. He secured Germany's first colonies, and is often presented as an enlightened colonialist, preferring diplomacy to brute force. Nachtigal died in 1885, at just 51, years before the worst German massacres. Yet there are no good colonialists — good cops are there to help the bad cops do their jobs.

And while many so-called explorers dedicated themselves to scientific research, one of the most popular fields for German colonialists was phrenology — the study of human skulls. This was supposed to prove the biological superiority of so-called Aryans. Forced labor at the concentration camps included cleaning off skulls to send to Germany. 3,000 skulls ended up at German museums or universities like the Charité hospital. Some of these now are being returned — others might turn up in Opa's trunk in the attic.

1.11. Carl Peters
Petersallee

An unassuming street cuts through Nachtigalplatz on its way to Rehberge park, with both sides filled by 1920s housing complexes. This is Petersallee, and two colonial street names intersect here. Carl Peters was Germany's Imperial Commissar for Eastern Africa from 1885–8, and his attempt to establish a German colony provoked a rebellion. A much bigger uprising broke out in 1905. German troops responded with a scorched earth policy, so that not even ruins would remain of villages that were suspected of supporting the rebels. They killed as many as 300,000 people.

Even among other colonialists, Peters was known for extreme brutality, earning the nickname "Hänge-Peters" (Hanging Peters). Mass murders were never a problem for Peters's reputation. But while an ideal functionary of the empire needs to be absolutely ruthless, he is also expected to maintain a certain distance to the cruelties, sitting in a room drinking tea and reading books in Ancient Greek. This was not Peters's style — he was a hands-on colonialist.

Peters exploited local women as concubines. When he suspected one woman of having a relationship with a servant, he had both of them hanged and their villages burned down. The resulting unrest caused a bit of a scandal in the metropolis, and Peters was recalled from his post. He was dragged before a Reichstag committee where the social democratic leader August Bebel attacked German colonial policy. Peters was dishonorably discharged and went into exile in London.

He was only rehabilitated in 1937 — by Adolf Hitler personally. The Nazis, with their new colonial ambitions, saw Peters as a model for the bloodthirsty administrators they needed. In 1937, they renamed Londoner Straße in the African Quarter to Petersallee. (The name London Street came from the English Quarter on the opposite side of Müllerstraße.) The Nazi propaganda minister Joseph Goebbels made a film about Peters in 1941: a bizarre fascist cowboy movie, with 300 Black prisoners of war forced to serve as extras.

This Nazi connection is why Petersallee was the first colonial street in Berlin to be renamed. Fifty years after its fascist christening, in 1987, it was changed from Petersallee, named after Carl Peters ... to Petersallee, named after Hans Peters, no relation.

The latter was a conservative politician and law professor. For many activists, this was not a satisfying solution — why have a street in the middle of the African Quarter named after a random white dude with no connection to Africa?

For many years, the district council resisted demands to rename the streets. As pressure mounted, they considered more non-renamings: Lüderitzstraße, named after the colonialist, could be changed to Lüderitzstraße, named after the city of Lüderitz (which is named after the colonialist). Nachtigalplatz could be named after a Nachtigall, with one more "l," which is German for a nightingale.

Fortunately, these ideas were rejected as well. In 2018, after numerous hearings with activists and historians, the district council voted on an impressive plan. The streets shouldn't just be given new names relating to Africa. They should still refer to crimes committed by German imperialism — but instead of honoring the perpetrators, they should commemorate people who fought back.

As a result, Lüderitzstraße will become Cornelius-Frederiks-Straße, named after a leader of the Nama resistance who was killed in the Shark Island concentration camp in 1907. Nachtigalplatz will be named after Rudolf Duala Manga Bell, a king in Cameroon who was hanged by the German authorities in 1904. Petersallee will be split in two. The front part will be called Anna-Mungunda-Allee: She was one of the first women in the Namibian independence movement and died in an uprising in Windhoek in 1959. The part behind the square will be the Maji-Maji-Allee, referring to the uprising in German East Africa in 1905–7.

While this decision was made in 2018, as of this writing almost three years later, not a single street sign has been replaced. Hopefully that will have changed by the time you look at it.

1.12. Columbiadamm Cemetery
Friedhof Columbiadamm — Columbiadamm 122–140

We have so far looked at colonial street names in Mitte and in Wedding. This should not create the impression that other parts of the city are better. Far from it: AfricaVenir compiled a list of colonial street names in Berlin and it runs to 26 pages!

The multicultural district of Neukölln has made a start in confronting this history. Wissmannstraße ran up from Hermannplatz next to Hasenheide park. It was named after Hermann Wissmann, another "explorer" who replaced Peters as Imperial Commissar for Eastern Africa. A statue of Wissmann at the University of Hamburg drew protests as early as 1961. In 1967, the statue was knocked over, but authorities set it back up. When it was toppled again the next year — this time in a public action by angry students — the city gave up. The statue was put in storage, and only taken out again for the exhibition on colonialism at the German Historical Museum in 2017 — where Wissman was shown lying on the ground and covered with spray paint.

Nonetheless: A prominent Neukölln street continued to honor Wissmann for another 60 years. In April 2021, it was renamed after Lucy Lameck, the first woman minister in independent Tanzania.

Taking Lucy-Lameck-Straße up the hill, we reach Columbiadamm, a street leading along the old Tempelhof airport. Past

Neukölln's public swimming pool, behind a red brick wall, stands Berlin's most militaristic cemetery. Statues of German soldiers from the Franco-Prussian War, World War I, and even World War II have jingoistic messages like "We died so that Germany may live!" The neighboring Turkish Cemetery was set up for Ottoman soldiers who died alongside their German allies — it still belongs to the Turkish Defense Ministry.

If we go to the back of the cemetery, against the eastern wall facing the pool, we will find a giant hunk of red granite: the Most Offensive Monument in Berlin! It is also dedicated to German soldiers. The colonial troops committing genocide against the Herero and Nama peoples themselves suffered some hardships, so this stone is dedicated to seven soldiers who "died a hero's death." And as if that weren't sufficiently atrocious, a logo of the German Afrika-Korps from 1941–3 was later added. This rock, created in 1907, was placed in the cemetery in 1973 and has stood here ever since.

A provisional plaque for the victims of the genocide was placed in front of the so-called Herero Stone in 2004. It disappeared after just a few days. A more permanent gravestone was installed in 2009 — now notably lacking the term "genocide." It was instead dedicated to the "victims of German colonial rule." And what can be said about it? If we wanted to be generous, we could say that the local politicians were doubtlessly well-intentioned. But the ensemble only serves to highlight the racism: While seven German murderers are honored with an enormous rock, their 60,000 victims are turned into the physical equivalent of a footnote.

The district council spent less than €2,000 for this lackluster marble slab. Every single year, more money is spent restoring the Africa Stone, which is semi-regularly defaced with paint. And yet, this insultingly inadequate marker remains the *only* monument to the victims of German colonialism anywhere in the country.

In 2020, as protesters around the world were knocking down statues of racists and colonialists, Berlin's Herero Stone escaped all public attention. This honestly does not speak well for Berlin's Left. The authors, editors, and publishers of this volume would never encourage or condone illegal behavior of any kind. We are just saying it is kind of weird that the rock is standing there so defiantly. The cemetery is almost completely empty. Anyone could enter, almost guaranteed to be unnoticed, every day between 8am and sundown. Alternatively, if a person wanted to go at night, they would not need to be very athletic to jump over the wall facing Columbiadamm and proceed the 20 meters or so to the rock — going in and out would probably take less than a minute. Plus, paint is cheap. It is weird, right?

1.13. Dahlem
Iltisstraße — Takustraße — Lansstraße

One Berlin neighborhood we will not be visiting in this guidebook is sleepy Dahlem, far in the southwest. When the city was divided, the Humboldt University ended up on the Eastern side, so the West established the Free University in 1948. With tens of thousands of students at FU, including the main leaders of the 1968 movement, Dahlem has seen its share of protests.

So far, we have only looked at German colonialism in Africa. The second Kaiser Wilhelm, who assumed the throne in 1888, focused on Asia and the Pacific. Northeast New Guinea was claimed as Kaiser-Wilhelmsland in 1884. Surrounding islands were also declared "protected areas" and given names like Neupommern, Neuhannover, and Neulauenburg. To this day, there is still a Bismarck Archipelago. Samoa was claimed as a German colony in 1900. In total, the German South Sea contained more than half a million colonial subjects.

Terrible massacres took place there as well. The pride of Berlin's Ethnological Museum (located in Dahlem for many years) was a Polynesian boat that was taken from the island of Luf in the Hermit Islands. New research has established that most of the 500 inhabitants of Luf were killed by the Germans. The Luf Boat, which is now on display in the rebuilt City Palace or Humboldt Forum, is thus a monument to genocide.

The German Empire also acquired a territory at Jiaozhou Bay in China. The lease was for 99 years — the same deal that Britain got for Hong Kong. When the so-called Boxer Rebellion began in 1900, the imperialist powers set aside their differences to subjugate China together. Wilhelm II gave a speech to German troops in Bremerhaven departing on the international punitive expedition. The 40-year-old Kaiser said:

Should you encounter the enemy, he will be defeated! No quarter will be given! Prisoners will not be taken! Whoever falls into your hands is forfeited. Just as a thousand years ago the Huns under their King Attila made a name for themselves, one that even today makes them seem mighty in history and legend, may the name German be affirmed by you in such a way in China that no Chinese will ever again dare to look cross-eyed at a German.

It is not that the Germans were more brutal than other colonial powers — but they did have a tendency to speak about their brutality more openly than the older, more refined empires. The British, who killed vastly more people in the colonies than the Germans could have dreamed of, held up the speech as an example of German barbarism. (This is, incidentally, why Germans in World War I were called "Huns.") The speech is a good riposte

Kaiser Wilhlelm II delivering his "Hun Speech" on July 27, 1900 in Bremerhaven to German troops departing for China. See Stop 1.13. Photographer unknown, but presumably Louis Koch. Via Wikimedia Commons.

to people who say that the crimes going on in the colonies were unknown in the metropolis.

Streets around the Free University commemorate the massacres. To enroll at the university, FU students have to go to a building on Iltisstraße, which they might assume is named after a European polecat (an iltis in German). It in fact honors the ship SMS Iltis that took part in the naval attack against the Taku Forts in China. That is in turn the source of the name Takustraße, which is where the John F. Kennedy Institute for North American Studies is located. The captain of the Iltis, Wilhelm Lans, is commemorated with Lansstraße. The Free University has been a center of the German student movement, full of anti-imperialist and anti-colonial ideas, since before 1968. How can these street names still be around?

Counterrevolutionary troops on top of the Brandenburg Gate during the so-called "Spartacist Uprising" on January 7, 1919. See Stop 2.10. Photographer unknown. Via Wikimedia Commons.

2

November Revolution

2.1. Potsdamer Platz
Pedestal in front of Potsdamer Platz 10

Potsdamer Platz is a soulless hub of corporate swagger — shiny towers erected in the 1990s when capitalism felt invincible. All the buildings are new, but the square has a long history. At the beginning of the twentieth century, it was dedicated to shopping — and by the end of the twentieth century, it had returned to form. From 1961–89, though, this was a flattened no man's land. Now, the wall has almost been forgotten among the shopping malls and chain stores.

As implausible as it seems, this is where the most important revolution in Berlin's history began. In 1916, the Great War had been going on for almost two years. The city was eerily quiet, as half of Germany's adult male population had been drafted into the army, and all strikes and demonstrations were prohibited. In the days before May 1, tiny slips of paper appeared all over the city. These advised: "Whoever is against the war will appear on May 1 at eight in the evening. Potsdamer Platz (Berlin). Bread! Freedom! Peace!"

A few thousand workers heeded the anonymous call. From the middle of the crowd, a 45-year-old man in a gray soldier's uniform lifted himself up. He had glasses, thinning hair, and a mustache. He might have held a short speech, but most people only heard two short bursts. "Down with the war!" he cried out. "Down with the government!"

As the demonstration was broken up, police dragged away the soldier. It was Karl Liebknecht. Not long ago, he had been a social democratic backbencher, but now he was Germany's most well-known parliamentarian. He wore soldier's gray because he had been drafted into the army a year earlier. When the Reichstag was in session, Liebknecht enjoyed immunity and could denounce the imperialist war in fiery speeches that were reported in all the newspapers. But as soon as the week's session closed, he was put on a train and sent to the front to dig trenches.

After the illegal demonstration, Liebknecht was put on trial for high treason on June 28, 1916. On that day, 50,000 metalworkers went on strike. They came from the AEG turbine factory in Moabit (which still stands as a factory for Siemens Energy at Huttenstraße 12–19) and many other munitions plants. Their demand was: "Freedom for Liebknecht!"

Liebknecht's mobilization on May 1 had been a brave yet helpless gesture, and he was sentenced to four years in prison. Paradoxically, this fiasco inspired the first mass workers' action against the war. The Liebknecht Strike had been organized by a group that was so secretive that they didn't even have a name. At the beginning of the war, elected workers' representatives from the factories started meeting because they wanted to fight for better working conditions, despite the bureaucrats' ban on strikes. Before long, this network (led by the lathe operator Richard Müller) radicalized, calling for an end to the war and to the monarchy. They became known by a descriptor: the Revolutionary Stewards.

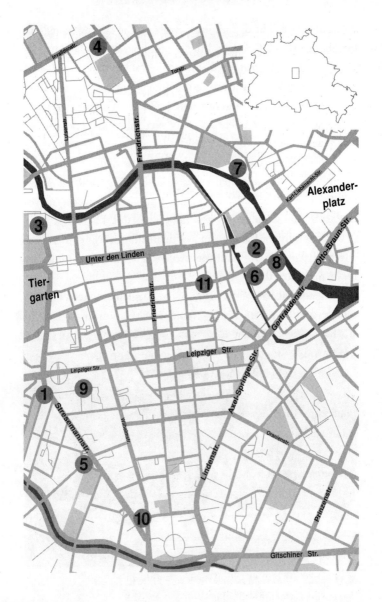

A curving red brick building stands on the southwest side of Potsdamer Platz. Columns lift the building above the entrance to the subway. A weathered stone pedestal stands in front, as if someone wanted to dismantle a monument but ran out of energy halfway. This marks the spot where Liebknecht's cry rang out.

In reality, the monument was only ever half-built. The pedestal was placed here by the East Berlin government on August 13, 1951, for Liebknecht's 80th birthday. It was dedicated by Friedrich Ebert — a name that will sound shocking until we realize that Friedrich Ebert had a son named Junior who served as mayor of East Berlin. A statue was never placed on top. There was going to be a big rally for Liebknecht's 90th birthday in 1961 — but just a few days before, the wall was erected, and the plinth ended up in the middle of the death zone.

The pedestal was removed in 1995 as Potsdamer Platz was being rebuilt, and then returned to its original location in 2002. The

In Memoriam of Karl Liebknecht, by Käthe Kollwitz. See Stop 9.4. Via Wikimedia Commons.

result is a kind of unintentionally postmodern non-monument. Normally, a bronze statue would try to convey the feeling that Liebknecht remains among us. These stones, in contrast, call out: No, Liebknecht is definitely gone, and not even dust remains. If you see him here, he is entirely in your mind. If he is to live on, it can only be by your deeds.

2.2. *City Palace*
Humboldt Forum — Schlossplatz

How old is this boxy, yellowish palace? Different dates can be given for its completion: 1451, 1702, 1853... In reality, though, this palace was completed in 2020 — and due to the pandemic, it did not open until 2021. The old City Palace once stood here — the Humboldt Forum is a brand-new copy. The former residence of the Hohenzollerns, the ruling dynasty of Brandenburg, Prussia, and the German Empire, was reconstructed at a cost of €600 million. This retrograde project was intended to connect Berlin to its aristocratic roots, as if the tumults of the twentieth century could be buried under columns and statues.

On July 31, 1914, the scion of the House of Hohenzollern, known as Kaiser Wilhelm II, gave a speech from the balcony above Portal V of the palace. The man with a handlebar mustache and a pompous uniform declared:

A momentous hour has struck for Germany. Envious rivals everywhere force us to legitimate defense. The sword has been forced into our hands. ... we shall show the enemy what it means to attack Germany.

In reality, Europe's Great Powers had been arming themselves to the teeth for more than a decade. Germany's general staff was prepared, in the words of one historian, to "grasp for world power." Yet this was not a popular cause. Just three days before the Kaiser's speech, hundreds of thousands of German workers had followed the call of the Social Democratic Party (SPD) and demonstrated for peace. That is why the German Kaiser — and all of Europe's monarchs — had to present their respective wars as defensive.

No one knew how the working class would react to the war. The SPD's leader of many decades, August Bebel, had died less than a year previously. He was remembered for his fierce opposition to the Franco-Prussian War in 1871. He had never wavered from his attitude: "I want to remain the mortal enemy of this bourgeois society."

In 1907, the Socialist International had resolved that in the case of war, all socialist parties were to "intervene in favor of its speedy termination and with all their powers to utilize the economic and political crisis created by the war to rouse the masses and thereby to hasten the downfall of capitalist class rule." In the summer of 1914, as the world inched ever closer to war, the SPD stuck to this principle, mobilizing its rank and file, and declaring: "We do not want war! Down with the war! Long live the international fraternization of peoples!"

On August 1, the day after the Kaiser's speech, Germany declared war on Russia. On August 4, the Reichstag was called together to vote on war credits. In Germany's barely constitutional monarchy, one of the parliament's few powers was controlling the budget. How would the SPD's 110 deputies vote?

Rosa Luxemburg, from the party's far left wing, was worried that they might not stick to their principles by voting no — she thought they might abstain.

2.3. Reichstag
Platz der Republik 1

Germany's parliament building gives architectural expression to the uneasy compromise between the aggressive monarchy and the toothless parliament established in 1871. It is an imposing fortress with a superficial dedication "to the German people." After the Reichstag was destroyed by a fire in 1933, the ruins sat empty during fascism and the Cold War. A glass dome, designed by Norman Foster, was placed on top in 1999, creating the seat of the Bundestag. This is a fitting symbol for the modern German state: high-tech decoration atop an autocratic structure inherited from the Kaisers.

Ironically, the Reichstag was the center of Germany's revolutionary movement for decades. Just three years after it was founded in 1875, the SPD was banned by the Socialist Laws (the English translation is more accurate: Anti-Socialist Laws). The party was forced to go underground: The leadership published its newspaper from Switzerland, while the members created a thick network of legal workers' associations dedicated to sports, education, hiking, singing, and every other activity. Such associations — as well as corner bars — provided cover for the illegal party. If "independent" candidates got elected to the Reichstag, they gained immunity and could therefore out themselves as

SPD representatives. The parliament thus became the only spot in Germany where the SPD could agitate under its own banner.

Social democracy grew continuously despite the ban, which had to be rescinded in 1890. By 1912, the SPD had become the largest party in Germany, with a million members, 4 million voters, 3 million members in affiliated unions, dozens of newspapers, and the largest faction in parliament. Over the decades, the SPD held on to the revolutionary Marxist principles of its founders — at least in theory. But as German capitalism grew ceaselessly, the working class won more and more reforms. The defeat of the Paris Commune in 1871 was followed by decades without revolutionary upheavals in Europe, and many wondered if the whole idea was an anachronism. The party would talk about the coming revolution and the socialist future on Sundays — but for the rest of the week, the SPD's work focused on union struggles and parliamentary reforms.

The war made this precarious balance between revolutionary theory and reformist practice impossible — was the SPD for or against? The German generals could offer threats: Did the socialists want to get banned again, and lose their newspapers, their union halls, and their parliamentary seats? But the officers had also studied their opponents: Had not Marx and Engels themselves called for a revolutionary war against the Russian Tsar as far back as 1848? Furthermore: Shouldn't socialists be willing to defend the limited democratic freedoms of the German Empire against the Tsarist autocracy?

The social democratic parliamentary faction met on August 3 for a pre-vote. Only 14 deputies wanted to vote no on war credits — the rest were in favor. Following the party's long tradition of "faction discipline," the 14 submitted to the majority. The Reichstag session the next day shocked the workers, if not the generals. SPD co-chair Hugo Haase, a well-known antimilitarist, gave the official speech: "In the hour of danger, we will not abandon our fatherland." Was there enthusiasm for the war, as has often been claimed? Students and petty-bourgeois sectors were certainly excited. In the working class, however, there was mostly confusion. For almost 50 years, the party had agitated against war — and now?

2.4. Liebknecht's Office
Chausseestraße 121

The war was supposed to be over by Christmas. Before long, however, millions of young men were stuck in trenches. The situation on the home front worsened from year to year. Working-class families went from potatoes to turnips to "bread" made of straw.

Despite talk of a "defensive" war, Germany immediately occupied neutral Belgium. The Kaiser's ministers began speaking openly about their plans for annexations. On December 2, 1914, after touring occupied Belgium and speaking with local socialists, Liebknecht became the first Reichstag deputy to vote against a second round of war credits. This was no defensive war: "It is an imperialist war, a war for the imperialist control of the world market." Liebknecht coined a slogan: "The main enemy is at home!"

By March of the following year, a second deputy, Otto Rühle, had voted no alongside Liebknecht. By January 1916, it was 20 deputies. Many of them were not from the party's left wing but from the center: They were not opposed to the war in principle, but they wanted the government to open peace negotiations. The SPD leadership expelled all 20 from the party. Soon, more and more SPD members were demanding a party congress. The party leadership expelled entire local organizations, and eventually a majority of the membership. Those who had been expelled formed the Independent Social Democratic Party (USPD) in April 1917.

Meanwhile, the revolutionary left wing of social democracy — including Luxemburg, Liebknecht, the feminist Clara Zetkin, and the historian Franz Mehring — were getting organized as well. In April 1915, they published a single issue of a magazine called *Die Internationale* — it was immediately banned. On January 1, 1916, they met at the law office of the brothers Karl and Theodor Liebknecht on the second floor* of the building at Chausseestraße 121 to found a new group. By September they were publishing an illegal leaflet called the *Spartacus Letters*, and thus the left became known as Spartacists. Their new group joined the USPD in order to have a legal framework, while maintaining their own program, publication, and organization.

There had long been three wings in German social democracy: a right wing based on the union bureaucracy that aimed to join the government of the imperialist state; a left wing that defended the party's revolutionary Marxist principles; and a center trying to hold the opposing wings together. These had once been three

---

* Attention, U.S. readers. Floors are listed here in European style, so the "first floor" is the first floor above the ground floor, which for you would be the second floor.

amorphous tendencies within the same party. As the war dragged on, they became opposing parties: Majority SPD (right), Independent SPD (center), and Spartacus (left).

A monument to the Spartacus Group, in the shape of a torch, was erected in 1958 behind an East German supermarket. Now, drab white condos have been built in front. You can ring the bell for "Denkmal" to enter the courtyard. The statue is inscribed with words that Karl Liebknecht wrote just days before his death: "Spartacus means the fire and the spirit, the heart and the soul, and the will and the deed of the proletariat's revolution." That provides a nice contrast to the *nouvelle riche* surroundings.

The building is just a few doors down from the Dorotheenstadt Cemetery. Lots of boring aristocrats and bourgeois are buried here, but you can also find graves of Germany's intellectual avant-garde: Bertolt Brecht (See Stop 7.3), John Heartfield, Georg Wilhelm Friedrich Hegel, Hanns Eisler (See Stop 4.6), Heinrich Mann, and Herbert Marcuse. That last one has an inscription on his grave that says, "Keep Going!"

2.5. *Berlin's Biggest Train Station*
Anhalter Bahnhof

The ruins in front of athletic fields and the Tempodrom arena are easy to overlook. The intricate brickwork and broken statues give only a hint of what a monumental building once stood here. Anhalter Bahnhof was the biggest train station in Berlin — the remaining portico is just half as tall as the arched hall once was.

Over the course of 1918, Germany's general staff was forced to recognize that their "grasp for world power" had failed.

Rather than admit defeat, they maneuvered to save what they could of their caste privileges. Knowing that the conditions for peace would be harsh, they created the myth that the German army had been "undefeated on the field of battle," but "stabbed in the back" by socialists, Jews, and other unpatriotic elements.

With Woodrow Wilson calling for democracy in Europe, the German generals attempted to make their dictatorship look a bit more liberal. When some political prisoners were amnestied on October 23, 1918, Liebknecht was allowed to return to Berlin. The city remained under a state of siege — there was to be no hero's welcome for the beloved antimilitarist.

Word spread, however, that Liebknecht would be arriving at Anhalter Bahnhof. Thousands of workers came to the station. Police formed a line at the entrance to prevent them from making it to the platform. But this was Berlin's busiest train station, with people coming and going constantly. So the cops started checking if people had tickets. Workers therefore bought tickets for the S-Bahn, as these were the cheapest.

When Liebknecht's train arrived, red flags, flowers, and throngs of cheering proletarians filled the platform to greet him. This is the source of the best joke about the German Revolution, variously attributed to Lenin or Stalin: "Revolution in Germany will never work. When these Germans want to occupy a train station, they first buy a platform ticket!"

Back in Berlin, Liebknecht joined the meetings of the Revolutionary Stewards. He pushed for a general strike and an uprising as soon as possible. One of their meetings, on November 2, took place in the back room of a bar on Neukölln's Boddinstraße — the address, unfortunately, has been lost to history. The Stewards reported that the mood in the factories was not ready for a showdown, and they demanded more time to prepare.

The German Revolution developed more quickly than German revolutionaries expected. It began in Kiel on the Baltic Sea and Wilhelmshaven on the North Sea. With the war essentially over, the German admiralty ordered the ships to sail out for a final — and totally hopeless — battle against the British fleet. The glorious deaths of tens of thousands of sailors would save their commanders' honor. The sailors were not interested — they raised red flags on their ships and arrested their officers. On November 4, after a general strike in Wilhelmshaven, a new body proclaimed that it had taken power in the city: the Workers' and Soldiers' Council.

The revolution crashed over Germany like a wave. The monarchies that made up the German Empire fell one after the other. Workers' and soldiers' councils were elected in city after city. But when would this movement reach Berlin, the heart of Prussian militarism and bureaucracy? The Revolutionary Stewards, after weeks of pressure from Liebknecht, agreed to set the date for a rising on November 11. Being very German revolutionaries, they typed up detailed plans for the insurrection — when one of their members was arrested, these files fell into the hands of the police. The date was hastily moved up to November 9. The call went out through the Stewards' underground network. The revolutionaries tried their best to prepare — with groups called "White Cats" distributing fliers and "Black Cats" gathering weapons — and then had to wait. By the end of November 9, they would either be in power or be dead.

2.6. State Council Building

former Staatsratsgebäude — ESMT — Schlossplatz 1

This eclectic building, just south of the City Palace, has a baroque entrance, laden with gold and statues, protruding from the otherwise clean lines of Stalinist modernism. This was once the State Council of the German Democratic Republic — after 1964, the country no longer had a president, and this body formed the collective head of state.

The back of the entrance hall is filled with a three-story stained-glass window designed by Walter Womacka. Ascending the spiraling stairs, we can follow the history of the German workers' movement: We start with abstract shapes representing oppression and ignorance. This is followed by red scenes of revolt, with sailors in blue uniforms and women in headscarves fighting under the visages of Luxemburg and Liebknecht. The massive piece is crowned by golden images of the fruits of the struggle: a happy proletarian family building up the workers' and peasants' state. It's kitschy, but impressive.

The conspicuous balcony is a remnant from the old City Palace. The palace was heavily damaged in the war, and the ruins were carted away in 1950, with bits ending up all over the city. The four bronze lions that once stood at the feet of a monument to Wilhelm I, for example, are now on display in front of the big cat house at the East Berlin Zoo. (See Stop 10.2) The Portal IV, however, was saved due to what happened here…

November 9 was a Saturday — a workday in imperial Germany. In the morning, workers gathered outside their factories. They marched into the city center from all directions. These columns were led by armed soldiers — photos of the insurrection invariably show men. But who was working in the factories while the men were at the front? Women. It was women who formed the backbone of the uprising.

The demonstrations went past military barracks and called on soldiers to join. The soldiers, however, had no idea what was going on, and with few exceptions they declared they would remain neutral. At the Maikäferkaserne (literally: the Beetle Barracks) on Chausseestraße, where the headquarters of Germany's Federal Intelligence Service (BND) now stands, officers fired into the crowd. Three workers were killed, including the 25-year-old toolmaker Erich Habersaath, the first martyr of the insurrection. Soon, throngs of workers filled the city center, surrounding every government building.

The Kaiser was not in Berlin — he was at army headquarters in occupied Belgium. His government was in the hands of Prince Max of Baden, a liberal aristocrat who had been appointed to carry out the peace negotiations. The new chancellor realized the only way to head off a revolution was for the Kaiser to abdicate the throne. He sent urgent messages to Wilhelm, but got only vague responses. By midday, Prince Max decided he could wait no longer, and proclaimed that the monarch had resigned. (In reality, the Kaiser fled to the Netherlands that evening, but only formally renounced the throne a month later.) Prince Max then resigned himself, and on the way out the door, named Friedrich Ebert from the SPD to replace him as chancellor. Ebert had recently said: "I hate the revolution like I hate sin." Now the revolution had put him in charge.

What kind of state would replace the crumbling Reich? Ebert and the other SPD leaders had been trying to convince one of the Kaiser's sons to assume the throne. Failing that, SPD leaders were considering some kind of regency. But the sea of people filling Berlin's streets would not be pacified with piecemeal reforms. A new era had already begun. Another leading social democrat, Philipp Scheidemann, proceeded to a window of the Reichstag and told the crowd: "The old and rotten has collapsed. Long live the new; long live the German Republic!" Ebert was incensed, telling his colleague: "You have no right to proclaim the republic!"

In reality, Scheidemann had no choice. Liebknecht had come into the city at the head of a demonstration from Schöneberg and was preparing to proclaim the republic himself. Just before 5pm, he climbed up to Portal IV of the palace, and called out: "The old is no more. The rule of the Hohenzollerns, who lived in this palace for centuries, is over. In this hour we proclaim the Free Socialist Republic of Germany."

The State Council Building now houses a private business school. Depending on who is working at the reception, they might let you inside to walk around. Otherwise you can book a tour on their website. Or you can check out the replica of Portal V at Humboldt Forum — Berlin now has two!

2.7. *Circus Busch*
James-Simon-Park — S-Bhf Hackescher Markt

This small triangular park, wedged between the Spree river and the elevated tracks of the S-Bahn, offers views of the back of the Pergamon Museum, as well as some tourist bars. This piece of land was once the site of a massive circus: Circus Busch, which opened in 1895, could seat over 4,000 people.

Germany's old order had been destroyed on a Saturday (November 9, 1918). On Sunday, it was time to build a new one. The suddenness was hard to process. As journalist Theodor Wolff put it:

a gigantic military organization seemed to embrace everything, in public offices and ministries an apparently invincible bureaucracy was enthroned. Yesterday morning all this was still there. ... Yesterday afternoon nothing remained.

The Revolutionary Stewards, meeting in the Reichstag in the evening after the insurrection, called for a general assembly of workers' and soldiers' councils the next day. Delegates elected in the factories and barracks were supposed to come to Circus Busch at 5pm. In reality, of course, it was impossible to check mandates, and the 3,000 workers and soldiers who filed in could have represented everyone or no one. The Stewards, basing themselves on their extensive network in the factories, planned to have themselves elected as the Executive Council of Workers' and Soldiers' Councils of Greater Berlin. Their conspiratorial leaders, however, were completely unknown to the masses. The SPD, meanwhile, had used its apparatus to visit different barracks and mobilize soldiers.

The assembly turned into a chaotic fight between the Stewards and the social democrats. Ebert and the SPD leadership had expelled everyone from their party who opposed the war. Now, they were making demagogic calls for "unity" among all workers' organizations. Many workers and soldiers, having awoken to political life only the previous day, did not yet understand the differences between the SPD, the USPD, and Spartacus. The soldiers at Circus Busch aggressively demanded "parity" — they wanted equal numbers of SPD and USPD members in the councils. (The Stewards and the Spartacists were all USPD members.) When Liebknecht tried to speak about how the SPD had betrayed socialism by supporting the war, he was booed off the stage. The assembly then confirmed a new provisional government with a revolutionary-sounding name — Council of People's Deputies — that included three ministers from the SPD and three from the USPD.

As one historian has pointed out, every proletarian revolution contains some kind of dual power, but the German Revolution might be the only case where one man — Friedrich Ebert — headed both the old and the new power. Ebert was both the Chancellor of the Reich Government (named by Prince Max) and simultaneously the strong man of the council government. This was possible because Ebert, like Janus, was presenting two different programs: In public, he was the top representative of the councils; in private, he established secret contact to the military headquarters and formed an alliance with General Wilhelm Groener to fight against the council system.

Years later, trying to justify his "revolutionary" rhetoric against right-wing critics, Ebert explained that the social democrats had understood that they needed to place themselves at the head of the movement — in order to cut off the movement's head at the appropriate time. They had done everything they could to stop the general strike on November 9 — but the night before, when they realized it would happen anyway, they put out a call for a general strike themselves.

2.8. New Marstall
Neuer Marstall — Schlossplatz 7

If we think of the City Palace as a house, then this building right behind it is the garage. The Marstall (there is both an "old" and a "new" one) was built for the court's horses and carriages — but it's rather fancy to be called a "stable." The GDR added some metal reliefs of Marx and Liebknecht, and today the building houses the Hanns Eisler School of Music.

On November 11, 1918, with the new government in place, rank-and-file sailors created an armed force to defend the revolution. Many of them had participated in the mutinies in Kiel and Wilhelmshaven. They were called to Berlin to protect public order in the capital.

With the war now officially over, Germany's military was melting away. Soldiers abandoned the trenches and set off toward home, often taking their weapons with them. The Ebert government would order companies to march into Berlin — but before they even reached the city limits, they had lost half their strength, and by the next morning they had disappeared entirely.

The People's Navy Division was founded to be a reliable force in turbulent times. The sailors set up their headquarters in the Marstall, and one of their first responsibilities was protecting the palace from looting. Soon they had over 3,000 armed men in the navy's typical blue uniforms with red armbands. The division's first commander was a bus driver and airplane mechanic named Paul Wieczorek. Just two days after he was elected by his comrades, he was shot and killed by a right-wing spy. Wieczorek's grave remains standing in the cemetery Friedhof IV der

Gemeinde Jerusalems- und Neue Kirche on Bergmannstraße in Kreuzberg.

The division was set up on Ebert's orders. But was it loyal to Ebert? The sailors' program declared:

> support for the government, which has fundamentally committed itself to the social republic. ... This unit will never allow itself to be used as a weapon of capital against the proletarians.

In reality, Ebert was trying to prevent socialism. The sailors were thus loyal to what the government said it wanted — and opposed to what the government actually did. Soon, Ebert became convinced that the People's Navy Division was controlled by subversives and Spartacists. He increasingly relied on proto-fascist paramilitary units called Freikorps.

The government told the People's Navy Division to demobilize, and stopped paying the sailors' wages. In response, they arrested the city commander from the SPD. Early in the morning of December 24, right-wing troops surrounded the palace and the Marstall. They started shooting with artillery and machine guns. Their command center was at the university across the street. Thousands of working people came out to support the sailors barricaded in the Marstall. The encirclers were thus encircled!

When shooting began, the civilians fled. An observer noted how these German proletarians, running for their lives through the imperial gardens, were careful to follow the zigzagging paths. This led to the second-best joke about the German Revolution, similarly attributed to Lenin or Stalin: "In Germany there can be no revolution, because that would require stepping on the grass."

After several hours, the right-wing troops were forced to retire, and the sailors held the palace and the Marstall. Eleven sailors had been killed, as well as several dozen mercenaries. Ebert claimed he didn't know who had ordered this counterrevolutionary operation. Nobody believed him — Rosa Luxemburg referred to the events as "Ebert's bloody Christmas." The Council of People's Deputies collapsed, with the USPD resigning in protest. Now only SPD members remained in the government. This is when Ebert dropped his revolutionary pretensions and began referring to himself as the Reich Chancellor. The government needed a war minister. An SPD bureaucrat named Gustav Noske volunteered: "Someone has to be the bloodhound," he said.

2.9. Berlin Parliament
Abgeordnetenhaus — Niederkirchnerstraße 5

This reddish hall has served many functions over the course of the twentieth century. It opened in 1899 as the seat of Prussia's House of Representatives. Under the Nazis, it was used by the bloodthirsty "People's Court." Since 1990, it has been Berlin's parliament building, replacing the Schöneberg City Hall.

A month after the revolution began, a national congress of workers' and soldiers' councils gathered here. When the delegates assembled in the great hall from December 12–16, 1918, images of the Kaiser were covered with red cloth. While the Independents and the Spartacists had plenty of support among Berlin's proletariat, this was not represented at the congress. Of the 485 delegates, a full 288 belonged to the SPD. The USPD had just 90, which included ten Spartacists. Paradoxically, a party opposed to the councils had the majority at the council congress. Germany's councils were not like the soviets in the Russian Revolution, which were made up of delegates elected in the factories and recallable at any time. In many German cities, a "council" was proclaimed on the day of the insurrection, made up of the local leaders of the different workers' organizations. As a result, delegates to Germany's national congress of councils were more likely to be politicians or lawyers than workers.

Luxemburg and Liebknecht, who had refused to sit next to Ebert on Berlin's council, had no mandate for the congress. Instead, Liebknecht mobilized 30,000 people outside the building. He climbed up to the balcony and gave a speech demanding "All power to the councils!" The proceedings of the congress were continuously interrupted by delegations of revolutionary workers and soldiers. They pressured the congress to pass radical resolutions about democratizing the army or socializing industry — these resolutions were never implemented. On the central question facing the congress, the SPD carried the day: Instead of founding a workers' republic based on councils, a big majority voted to hold a National Assembly based on universal suffrage. The date for electing the assembly was set in two months' time. The councils thus relinquished power — a "political suicide club," as one participant called it.

The Spartacists had been part of the USPD since 1917. At least a third of USPD members in Berlin supported the revolutionary left. But the party leadership refused to call a congress before the elections. Spartacist leaders, especially Luxemburg and Leo Jogiches, had been hesitant to leave the USPD. The results of the congress convinced them that they needed their own party in order to provide a revolutionary leadership for the working class, independent of the USPD's constant wavering.

On December 30, 1918, the Spartacists invited delegates from across Germany to the founding congress of a new party. The Communist Party of Germany (KPD) was born on the first day of 1919. The three-day meeting took place in the ballroom of the Berlin parliament, which is above the main entrance on the top floor. The room is sometimes accessible to the public, but it is totally unremarkable today, and nothing but a cheap sign notes that the KPD was created here. The USPD had hundreds of thousands of members, and only a tiny fraction of them joined the new communist party.

2.10. SPD Headquarters
Wilhelmstraße 140

Today, the Social Democratic Party has its headquarters where Wilhelmstraße meets Stresemannstraße. The Willy-Brandt-Haus — reminiscent of a ship and named after the former West Berlin mayor and West German chancellor — opened in 1999. At the time, Germany's social democrats had just won an election with 40% of the votes. But after applying brutal austerity measures, their support collapsed and has never recovered. The SPD, once Germany's largest party, now has to rent out large parts of its headquarters just to pay the bills.

The original party headquarters is just 500 meters away. We can follow the small Franz-Klühs-Straße heading east: where it intersects with Lindenstraße, three metal signs mark the spot. A row of buildings at Lindenstraße 2–4 housed the SPD's national headquarters, the editorial offices and printing presses of its Berlin newspaper *Vorwärts*, the bookshop, and the party university. It was known as the *Vorwärts* building.

(The exact location is rather confusing: We have to imagine that Lindenstraße once led directly into Mehringplatz, which was called Belle-Alliance-Platz, rather than curving around it. The SPD occupied a number of buildings on the eastern side of Lindenstraße, just off the square. The historical markers are thus too far to the north-east — where the entrance of the *Vorwärts* building once stood, there is now a garden behind Mehringplatz 9 in the circular housing projects.)

As the year 1918 came to a close, Ebert and Noske understood that their government did not have a strong social base. Their hope lay in provocation: They needed to draw the revolutionary movement into a decisive battle before it could organize its forces. This is why they fired Emil Eichhorn on January 4, 1919.

Eichhorn was Berlin's revolutionary police chief, which sounds like an oxymoron. Eichhorn was no cop — he was in fact a socialist journalist who led the occupation of Berlin's police headquarters during the insurrection of November 9. The "Red Castle," as the massive building was known, once loomed over Alexanderplatz. Its place has been taken by the pink shopping mall Alexa — one symbol of capitalist domination replacing another...

On that day, Berlin police abandoned their weapons and uniforms without a fight, and Eichhorn established a new police force. Two months later, the revolutionary police chief represented one of the last remaining conquests of the revolution. For the SPD, Eichhorn was an obstacle to their counterrevolutionary "order." When the government attacked the People's Navy Division, for example, Eichhorn's police had fought alongside the sailors. He rejected his firing, stating: "I received my position from the revolution, and I will only return it to the revolution!"

The Revolutionary Stewards, the USPD, and the KPD called for a demonstration to defend Eichhorn on January 5. The response was enormous: Up to half a million people took to the streets — more than on November 9. The strike committee decided that the masses were on their side, and it was time to topple the Ebert government once and for all. They reconstituted themselves as a Revolution Committee of 53 members, led by Liebknecht, George Ledebour, and Paul Scholze, and declared they had taken power. That day, armed workers marched to Berlin's newspaper district and occupied a number of newspapers, including the *Vorwärts*.

On January 6, the general strike continued, as massive as before. Only a few thousand came to a rally in support of the Ebert government in front of the Reich Chancellery. But the Revolution Committee, which had proclaimed that it was the new government, took no measures. They lacked even the most basic organization to exercise power. They sent 200 sailors to occupy the War Ministry. At the door, the commander presented an order signed by Liebknecht. The doorman examined the paper and pointed out that it had a signature, but lacked a stamp. Therefore, he could not hand over the building. The sailors turned around to get better paperwork — and never returned.

Things like that happened all over the city. The masses were ready to fight, but got no instructions from their leaders. By the third day, the strike front began to crumble. Workers had been standing in the cold for two days. This is the moment that Ebert and Noske had been waiting for. Now they ordered the Freikorps into the city. The paramilitaries only had 30,000 men, but they were well organized and heavily armed. They moved from one workers' district to the next, murdering anyone they identified as a "Spartacist."

Fighting soon concentrated around the *Vorwärts* building. Up to 300 workers were inside, armed with a few rifles and a machine gun. The Freikorps surrounded them on January 10, and attacked the next morning with grenade launchers, flame throwers, and even a British tank. A delegation of seven occupiers tried to negotiate a surrender. They were arrested and taken over the canal to the Guards Dragoon Barracks (the Garde-Dragoner-Kaserne at Mehringdamm 20-28, which today houses the Kreuzberg tax office).

The seven negotiators were all beaten to death. Soon, the remaining occupiers had to surrender unconditionally. They were taken to the same barracks, expecting to be mowed down with machine guns. Yet they survived — perhaps no commander could be found who dared to order such a large execution. At this time, Luxemburg and Liebknecht went into hiding. We will trace their steps in the next chapter.

2.11. Murder of the Sailors
Französische Straße 32

This simple yet tasteful white building houses a fancy capitalist foundation. Nothing recalls the cold-blooded massacre that took place here.

During the attempted insurrection in January, the People's Navy Division had effectively split. Some sailors fought alongside the workers; others remained at their posts protecting the Reichstag, the Chancellery, the Reichsbank, and other centers of power; the commanders attempted to remain neutral.

After the uprising was defeated, the SPD forced the sailors out of the Marstall. They set up a new headquarters at the Navy House a kilometer down the banks of the Spree river. The building at Märkisches Ufer 48-50 was once a clubhouse for a navy unit. Since 1980, a worn-down plaque has commemorated the People's Navy Division. Today, the mostly empty building houses a seafood restaurant.

On March 11, 1919, the People's Navy Division was dissolved. The sailors were told to report to an office at Französische Straße 32 to receive their final wages. One by one, 250 sailors arrived. Inside the building, they were disarmed and detained by reactionary troops under the command of Otto Marloh. Marloh selected about 30 sailors at random and led them down to the courtyard. They were stood against a wall and executed with machine guns. A single sailor survived the massacre by playing dead among the corpses.

At the end of the year, Marloh was placed on trial for the mass murder of the sailors. He was acquitted because he could claim that he had only been following Noske's orders. The war minister and self-described bloodhound had declared: "Every person who is seen fighting against government troops with weapons in hand is to be shot immediately." And of course, if a paramilitary wanted to shoot anyone, he could always claim they were holding a weapon (or had been in a building from which gunshots had been heard).

In March 1919, another general strike shook Berlin. The Freikorps, under orders from the SPD, attacked working-class neighborhoods with artillery, tanks, planes, and poison gas. By Noske's own estimates, 1,200 so-called "Spartacists" were massacred without so much as courts martial, let alone actual trials. Modern historians estimate there were closer to 2,000 dead, including women and children.

The massacres of 1919 were not the end of the German Revolution. There were further general strikes and insurrections in the Ruhr region and in Central Germany. There were short-lived council republics in Bremen in the North and Munich in the South. But the revolution still lacked a real leadership. The centralized power of the social democracy and the military was able to put down each rising individually.

The far right terminated their alliance with the SPD in 1920 and attempted a putsch against Ebert. The SPD government fled Berlin and called for a general strike — the first and only national general strike in Germany's history. Ten million workers followed the call, shutting down the whole country. This toppled the Kapp Putsch in three days. The reinstalled SPD government immediately amnestied all the coup plotters and resumed repression against the working class.

This was the beginning of the bourgeois republic in Germany. The SPD was able to preserve "order," as they called it. But in reality, they saved the officer corps, the state bureaucracy, and above all the capitalists. They did this by arming proto-fascist paramilitaries to the teeth and giving them free rein to massacre proletarians. The SPD thus paved the way for these fascist forces to take power in Germany just 14 years later. Rosa Luxemburg has been correct: The choice was between socialism and barbarism. The social democrats were able to prevent socialism — with Nazi barbarism.

Rosa Luxemburg with Kostja Zetkin on the balcony of her apartment at Cranachstraße 58 in Friedenau in 1907 or 1908. See Stop 3.4. Photographer unknown. Via Wikimedia Commons.

3

Rosa Luxemburg's Berlin

3.1. In the Hansaviertel
Cuxhavener Straße 2

"Berlin has made the most unfavorable impression on me." It was 1898 and Rosa Luxemburg had just arrived in the capital of the German Empire. In a letter, she described the city as "cold, tasteless, massive — a real barracks; and the dear Prussians with their arrogance, as though every one of them had swallowed the stick with which they had once been beaten." She nonetheless remained here for the next two decades. Today, she is one of the city's most famous residents — there are dozens of monuments to her in both East and West.

During the lifetime of great revolutionaries, the oppressing classes constantly hounded them, received their theories with the most savage malice, the most furious hatred and the most unscrupulous campaigns of lies and slander. After their death, attempts are made to convert them into harmless icons, to canonize them, ... while at the same time robbing the revolutionary theory of its substance, blunting its revolutionary edge and vulgarizing it. — V.I. Lenin

Today, Rosa Luxemburg has the great misfortune that everyone loves her — or at least claims to. We can ask an individualist anarchist living in a shack in the woods and growing their own potatoes. We can ask a reformist government minister carrying out privatizations. We can ask a thuggish Stalinist praising North Korea. The one thing they will all agree on: They love, love, *love* Rosa Luxemburg.

This is ironic. During her lifetime, many people *hated* the Red Rosa. This tour will attempt to rescue her from canonization.

When she arrived in Berlin, Luxemburg was just 27, but already an experienced revolutionary. She had joined the socialist movement at 15 while still in school in her native Poland, which was then part of the Tsarist Empire. But like anyone who aspired to be a leader of the workers' movement under Tsarism, she had to go into exile. She moved to Switzerland and earned a doctorate in economics from the University of Zurich — she was among the first women in Europe with a PhD. In Zurich, Luxemburg met Leo Jogiches and the two founded their own group, the Social Democracy of the Kingdom of Poland and Lithuania (SDKPiL) (See Stop 4.5). Luxemburg decided that she needed to go to Berlin to be near the center of the international socialist movement. She acquired German citizenship via a fake marriage. As soon as she arrived in the city, Luxemburg went to the secretary of the Social Democratic Party (SPD), Ignaz Auer. She got a job as an agitator (today we would say: election campaigner) among the Polish-speaking workers of Poznan´ and Upper Silesia, then part of Prussia.

Before that, however, she needed a place to stay. In her first days in Berlin, she visited 75 different rooms before she finally found one at Cuxhavener Straße 2 in the Hansaviertel — a familiar experience for many new arrivals in Berlin today! The apartment was right next to Berlin's biggest park, the Tiergarten, where Luxemburg went for walks every day. She stayed there for almost one year until her landlady kicked her out. The building is no longer there — it stood on the eastern side of the train tracks, where the street has been reduced to a small path. The only building from that time belongs to the Honduran Embassy at Cuxhavener Straße 14. Just a few doors down is the GRIPS Theater, founded in the 1960s to provide anti-authoritarian musical theater for children and young people, and still going strong today.

Another resident of the Hansaviertel was Mathilde Jacob, who lived one block north at Altonaer Straße 11 (roughly where the Gymnasium Tiergarten is today, at Altonaer Straße 26). Jacob worked as a typist and translator. The two women first met in December 1913 when Luxemburg came to Jacob's apartment to give dictation for the *Sozialdemokratische Korrespondenz*. That newspaper was published by a trio from the radical left wing of the SPD: Luxemburg, Julian Marchlewski (known as "Karski"), and Franz Mehring.

Jacob would come to play a central role in Luxemburg's life. She was more than a close friend and a cat sitter: When Luxemburg was in prison, Jacob smuggled her extensive writings to the outside world. In the late 1930s, two decades after Luxemburg's murder, Jacob again saved her legacy by handing her papers over to a representative of the Hoover Institution. Jacob was able to save the documents, but not herself: She was deported to the concentration camp Theresienstadt in 1942 and died the following year.

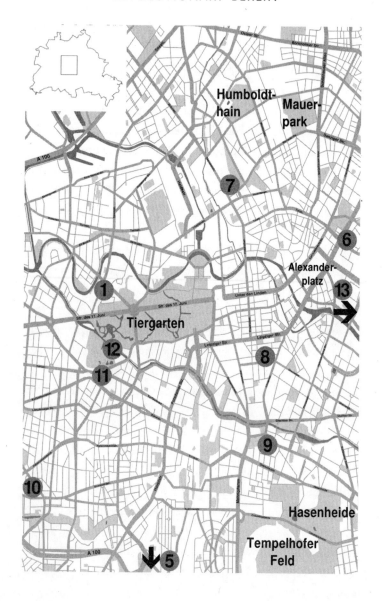

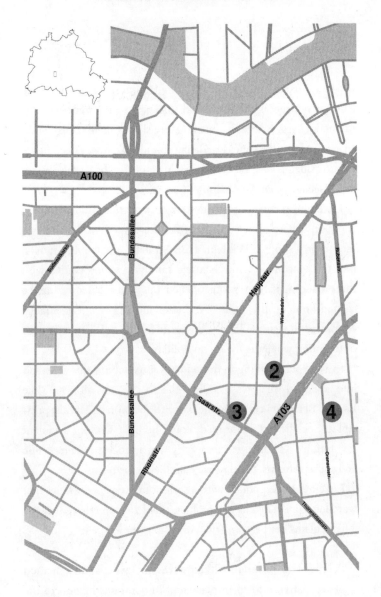

3.2. In Friedenau I
Wielandstraße 23

In 1899, Luxemburg moved from the Hansaviertel to Friedenau, a breezy bourgeois neighborhood emerging on the southern edge of Schöneberg, where the bustling city slowly melted into fields. In stories from the time, Friedenau sounds like it was deep in the countryside. Today, however, it is just outside the S-Bahn Ring, and bisected by an Autobahn.

Luxemburg ended up in this kiez because she could not find a room anywhere else — again, a familiar experience! After two months in a room at Wihlelm-Huff-Straße 4, Luxemburg moved into the apartment of the Neufeld family: a young couple with three daughters. Her room opened up to the balcony on the second floor on the right. Even after moving out, Luxemburg continued to visit the family, buy gifts for the kids, and take care of their dog while they were on holiday.

In 1900, while living in this address, Luxemburg threw herself into a debate that was rattling the SPD. "Revisionists" like Eduard Bernstein called on the party to abandon its Marxist principles. Socialism, they argued, could be built without a violent revolution — all that was necessary was a process of democratic and social reforms. (Today, we call this "reformism.")

Luxemburg responded with a series of newspaper articles that were later published as a pamphlet, titled *Reform or Revolution?*. This remains her best-known work. In it, she argued:

People who pronounce themselves in favor of the method of legislative reform in place and in contradistinction to the conquest of political power and social revolution, do not really choose a more tranquil, calmer and slower road to the same goal, but a different goal. Instead of taking a stand for the establishment of a new society they take a stand for surface modifications of the old society.

Since 2013, the building at Wielandstraße 23 has had a plaque about its former inhabitant. The ground floor is occupied by a daycare center (a "KiTa" in German). Luxemburg long desired to have a baby. She may have decided that as a woman at that time and in that society, a child would prevent her from fulfilling her duties to the revolutionary movement. Or perhaps she was just unable. In either case, she got a cat instead.

While working at the SPD headquarters, Luxemburg discovered a gray cat. She took the animal home, nursed it to health, and named it Mimi. The cat became her constant companion. Jacob took the animal when its owner went to prison. Luxemburg's letters from her cell alternate between brilliant analyses of world events and insistent queries about Mimi.

Perhaps the saddest episode of Luxemburg's life is when Mimi fell ill and died, and Jacob did not dare to write down the sad news. After a number of detailed questions about the animal received only vague answers, Luxemburg realized that something was amiss. Her cat had been dead for four months and no one had told her. She ultimately forgave Jacob and found new animals to love. From her cell, Luxemburg was still able to interact with birds, and included feathers with her letters.

3.3. *The Kautskys*
Saarstraße 14

This sturdy villa made of yellow bricks was once the intellectual center of the international socialist movement: the home of Karl and Luise Kautsky. Karl Kautsky edited the SPD's theoretical weekly, *Die Neue Zeit* (The New Times). As the world's most prominent Marxist after the death of Friedrich Engels, he was called the "Pope of Marxism."

Luxemburg and Kautsky were allies in the fight against revisionism. But as the first decade of the twentieth century progressed, their paths diverged. Luxemburg was sharply critical of the bureaucracy that was growing in the SPD and its affiliated unions. She was convinced that Prussian absolutism could not be overcome by reforms. Inspired by the Russian Revolution of 1905, she argued that the SPD should prepare for mass strikes like the ones that had shaken the Tsarist Empire. This was totally unacceptable to the bureaucrats running the unions, for whom the "general strike" was just "general nonsense."

With social democracy divided into irreconcilable wings, Kautsky's goal was to maintain party unity at any price. He was willing to criticize reformism in theory, but carefully avoided any resolutions that would antagonize the union bosses. Kautsky believed that the party could take power by winning a majority of seats in the Reichstag — but for this, both the left and right wings needed to stick together.

The Russian Revolution of 1905 radicalized many socialists in Germany. Luxemburg travelled to Warsaw to take part in the battle and ended up in a Tsarist prison. Kautsky, too, began thinking that revolution could spread from the East to the West. By the end of the decade, however, Kautsky had drifted back to the right. A final break between the two came in 1910.

That year, a mass movement broke out in Prussia. Hundreds of thousands of workers took part in illegal demonstrations to demand equal voting rights. Rosa Luxemburg thought the SPD should push the movement forward by agitating in favor of mass strikes. Kautsky, in contrast, believed the party needed to prepare for the next elections, set to take place in less than two years. Kautsky warned that calling for strikes would be too dangerous — it could lead to the party being prohibited again and losing everything it had built up over 40 years. Luxemburg responded: Why had they built such an apparatus, if not to provide leadership to mass actions that could topple the capitalist state? Kautsky argued that a policy of mass action would only be applicable in a revolutionary situation, whereas they were clearly in a non-revolutionary situation. Luxemburg countered that they could not look at the situation as an objective phenomenon, like sticking a hand out the window to check for rain. If a socialist party with a million members is calling for mass strikes, or if it is instead telling people to go home and wait for elections — is that not, in itself, part of the difference between a revolutionary and a non-revolutionary situation?

This is an attempt to summarize multiple books worth of polemics in just a few lines. Rosa Luxemburg criticized Kautsky's policy of passive waiting as "nothing-but-parliamentarism." As a result, she was barred from publishing her views in Kautsky's journal or in leading SPD newspapers. She never spoke to Karl Kautsky again. She did remain close with Luise Kautsky for the rest of her life. In fact, some of Luxemburg's best polemics against Karl Kautsky are contained in private letters to his wife.

In 1907, leading socialists met up at the Kautsky's house for dinner. Luxemburg and her friend Clara Zetkin had gone on a long walk and arrived late. Bebel joked that they had "feared the worst." To which Luxemburg replied that in the case of an accident, the gravestones of her and Zetkin should read: "Here lie the last men of German social democracy."

Today, this building is the headquarters of Germany's social democratic scouting organization, Die Falken (The Falcons). Except: Although this is called the Kautsky House — with a plaque, a sign, and an exhibition dedicated to the couple — there has been a misunderstanding. The Kautsky family did live at Saarstraße 14 from 1900–02, but the street was later renumbered. They actually lived in an apartment one block away: The new address (with a new building) is Saarstraße 19. They then moved a few blocks to Wielandstraße 26. This mistake has been repeated endlessly since the plaque was installed in 1980, including by this author. It was, admittedly, a bit strange to think the chief theoretician of social democracy would live in a huge mansion like this.

3.4. In Friedenau II
Cranachstraße 58

In 1902, Luxemburg moved into her own place at Cranachstraße 58: the apartment on the second floor on the right side of this red-trimmed castle. She remained here for nine years — the longest she stayed in one apartment in Berlin. At first, she and Jogiches lived here together — except he was officially her renter, as she was still legally married, and adultery was a crime. Luxemburg was earning more money as a journalist and Jogiches came from a wealthy family, so these two passionate communists had a series of live-in maids. Luxemburg sounds like a despicable boss — everyone, even a revolutionary, is a mess of contradictions.

The political couple split up in 1907, and Luxemburg began a relationship with Kostja Zetkin, her best friend's son. At 21, he was 14 years her junior. Zetkin even moved into the apartment for a time, even though the liaison had to remain secret. When he found out, Jogiches threatened to kill Zetkin, Luxemburg, and himself — Luxemburg took the threat seriously enough that she bought a pistol. Yet despite his abusive behavior, the two remained a team. During the war, Jogiches made sure that Luxemburg's writings were distributed throughout Germany. When the revolution arrived, she hardly made a decision without consulting him. (See Stop 4.5)

In 1907, Luxemburg began working as a teacher at the SPD's party university, located at their headquarters at Lindenstraße 2–4. (See Stop 2.10) Party officials from across the Empire were sent here for a six-month course to learn Marxist theory, workers' history, and economics. Fellow teachers included Franz Mehring, a gray-bearded historian who was also on the party's far-left wing (and today serves as the patron of the Mehringplatz in Kreuzberg). One of her students was Friedrich Ebert — who went on to murder her, but we will get to that presently.

In the 1980s, a brothel opened at Cranachstraße 58 with the name "Rosa L." This was the height of the autonomist women's movement in West Berlin, and soon a brick flew through the window. The name was changed.

In contrast to the other address in Friedenau, there is no plaque on this building. When one was to be installed in the 1970s, the owner resisted for a decade. So a parking spot was removed and a freestanding metal sign was set up there. If you know how Germans feel about parking spots, you can imagine that this almost led to an insurrection.

3.5. In Südende
Biberacher Weg 2

In 1911, Luxemburg moved to Südende, a 40-minute walk further south. This is a very sleepy residential neighborhood. I should admit that after decades in Berlin, the only time I have ever been here is to search for Luxemburg's former address. One could also visit the National Railway Agency and the Vodafone headquarters for Eastern Germany.

Luxemburg, her maid, and her cat all moved into a five-room apartment in the attic of a single-family home on Lindenstraße (not to be confused with the street of the same name in Kreuzberg). This street is now called Biberacher Weg. She moved to a suburb, surrounded by fields and fresh air, to write her opus, *Accumulation of Capital: A Contribution to an Economic Explanation of Imperialism*, in which she attempted to develop Marx's ideas for the age of imperialism.

Südende is where she began collecting plants. Today you can get a reprint of her *Herbarium*, with over 400 pages of leaves and flowers that Luxemburg pressed and labelled. She would later recall, in a letter to Sophie Liebknecht, walking through the fields of Südende:

Deep down I feel much more at home in a small garden ...
or in a meadow with bumblebees and grass than — at a party
congress. I can tell you all this: you will not promptly suspect
me of treason to socialism. ... But my innermost self belongs
more to my birds than to the comrades.

When she had to enter prison in 1915, her friends were able to
keep the apartment for her. She did return three years later — but
she only spent a few restless nights in Südende, as the revolution
kept her in constant motion. Her refuge was gone. Once, returning home after working in the editorial offices of *Die Rote Fahne*
until after midnight, she told Jacob:

Can you tell me why I am always living in a state to which I do
not have the slightest inclination? I want to paint and live on a
patch of earth where I can feed animals and love them. I want
to study natural sciences. Above all I want to live peacefully by
myself, and not in this endless hustle.

When the revolution reached Südende, Luxemburg was elected
onto the workers' council of Mariendorf. Under the leadership of
fellow Spartacist Hugo Eberlein, the council briefly took power
in the small town.

The old house is gone — an ugly single-family home stands
in its place. The district government has yet to put up a marker.

3.6. Women's Prison
Barnimstraße 10, at the corner of Weinstraße

This part of Friedrichshain is full of monotonous but functional Stalinist housing blocks. Not even an outline remains of the Berlin Women's Prison, which opened its gates in 1864.

In 1913, as war raged in the Balkans, Luxemburg had called on the workers' movement to oppose a new imperialist conflagration. "If we are called on to raise murder weapons against our French or other foreign brothers" she thundered, "then we will declare: No, we refuse!" For this speech at two anti-war rallies in Frankfurt am Main, she was convicted of "Incitement to Disobey Laws and Orders of the Authorities."

Her lawyer Paul Levi appealed the sentence, so she was still free when World War I began and the SPD voted for war credits on August 4, 1914. That evening, the party's radical left wing gathered at her apartment in Südende to discuss their response. They sent 200 telegrams across the Empire inquiring who would be prepared to join a public protest — the only positive response came from Clara Zetkin in Stuttgart. Luxemburg thought she might have to commit suicide to make her voice heard.

On February 18, 1915, Luxemburg had to enter the prison in Friedrichshain. This is where she wrote the pamphlet *The Crisis of German Social Democracy*, calling for the refoundation of the Socialist international. Mathilde Jacob smuggled out the manuscript, which was eventually published in Zurich. As it appeared under the pseudonym "Junius," it became known as the "Junius pamphlet." In April 1915, Luxemburg's friends published a single issue of a new magazine, *Die Internationale*, which was immediately confiscated by the military authorities.

After exactly one year, she was able to return to Südende — but only briefly. She joined Karl Liebknecht at the May Day

The "citizens' militia" posing outside the building where they arrested Rosa Luxemburg and Karl Liebknecht on January 15, 1919. Note the steel helmets, rifles, and hand grenades. See Stop 3.10. Photographer unknown. Via Wikimedia Commons.

rally at Potsdamer Platz. (see Stop 2.1) When her comrade was arrested, she "tried to liberate him with all the force of my fists," but she was unsuccessful. In July 1916, as the first mass workers' actions against the war began, Luxemburg and other revolutionary leaders were rounded up. Now she was put into "protective custody" — which sounds like she was to be protected, but in fact the state was protecting itself from her. This meant she was imprisoned indefinitely without trial, spending the rest of the war in fortresses in Poznań and Breslau (which are today in Poland).

Luxemburg's friends founded an underground organization on the first day of 1916, and in September they published their first illegal flyer. (See Stop 2.4) The journalist Ernst Meyer was in charge of getting it printed, and thinking about the slave revolt in ancient Rome, he picked the name "Spartacus." Liebknecht had given a green light, but at the group's next meeting, no one was happy with the name. The *Spartacus Letters* were such an immediate success, however, that the name was impossible to change. Luxemburg was stuck with it for the rest of her life — even until today.

The women's prison was torn down in 1974. Today the lot contains simulated streets where kids are taught how to ride bicycles. (It's a German thing.) In 1977, a monument in the shape of prison bars was placed opposite the entrance to a school. An additional, more recent plaque is dedicated to women resistance fighters against fascism, including Olga Benario, who were imprisoned here. (See Stop 4.7)

3.7. Northern Train Station
former Nordbahnhof — Wartehalle — Julie-Wolfthorn-Straße 1

While Luxemburg was stuck in prison, the long-awaited revolution finally arrived. Except it didn't start in Berlin — it began in Petrograd (which was founded as St. Petersburg and later changed to Leningrad, before becoming St. Petersburg again). The 500-year-old dynasty of the Romanovs was toppled in early March 1917. Germany's general staff celebrated — they hoped Russia's new government would be too weak to continue the war.

Ulrich von Brockdorff-Rantzau, the German ambassador to Denmark, developed a plan to create "the greatest possible chaos" in Russia. Numerous Russian revolutionaries were in exile in Switzerland. The Alpine nation had once offered them protection from Tsarist repression — but now they wanted to get back home as soon as possible to join the revolution, and they were surrounded by warring countries. The German government offered them safe passage, hoping to destabilize the enemy camp.

Negotiations were opened with all the different factions of the Russian revolutionary movement: Bolsheviks, Mensheviks, the Jewish Bund, and followers of Leon Trotsky. Conditions were agreed: The revolutionaries would take a train across German territory, but their car would remain sealed the entire time, so as not to create the impression the passengers were collaborating with imperialism.

The train left Zurich on April 9. Two days later, it stopped over in Berlin for 20 hours. No one got on or off. The train first parked at Potsdamer Bahnhof, then at Stettiner Bahnhof (which is today

Nordbahnhof). Of the once mighty train hall, only an underground S-Bahn station and a small yellow brick waiting room remain. The latter is now a private event space called Wartehalle. This is where the Russian Revolution briefly passed through Berlin. A few hours after departing the city, the revolutionaries reached the end of the line at a Baltic Sea port. They boarded a ferry to Stockholm, and then took sleighs to the Finnish border. After a week of travel, Locomotive #293 drove them into Petrograd.

Just seven months later, the workers and soldiers' councils took power in Petrograd. Lenin and Trotsky stood at the head of a soviet government. The October Revolution filled Luxemburg with enthusiasm. She had, after all, spent her entire life fighting against the Tsarist regime.

While Karl Kautsky accused the Bolsheviks of creating a brutal dictatorship that had nothing to do with socialism, Luxemburg's views were more complex. Still in prison, she wrote a pamphlet *On the Russian Revolution*. One single line is always quoted: "Freedom is always the freedom of those who think differently." This is interpreted as a denunciation of the Bolshevik government.

If we actually read the pamphlet, however, we find a ton of criticisms: on the national question, on agricultural policy, on freedom of the press, etc. But just below that one famous line, Luxemburg also wrote:

> It is not a matter of this or that secondary question of tactics, but of the capacity for action of the proletariat, the strength to act, the will to power of socialism as such. In this, Lenin and

Trotsky and their friends were the first, those who went ahead as an example to the proletariat of the world; they are still the only ones up to now who can cry …: 'I have dared!'

Luxemburg was a critical supporter of the Russian Revolution. And she never published that pamphlet — perhaps she simply never got around to it, as she only had two months after her release from prison. Or perhaps her views evolved, based on her own experiences with revolution. In a letter to Luise Kautsky, she wrote:

Are you not delighted with the Russians? They will of course not be able to maintain their power in this witches vigil — not because statistics show a backward economic development of Russia, as your clever husband has figured it out, but because the Social Democrats of the highly developed West are a lot of downright cowards and will passively look on now as the Russians are being bled to death.

In other words: Whatever problems Luxemburg saw with the workers' government in Russia, she placed the blame for them at the feet of reformists and centrists in Germany. She added that even if the revolution were defeated, "It is a world-historic deed, the imprints of which will not be obliterated by the passing of ages." She understood that revolution would demand sacrifices, bloodshed, and even brutality from the working class. But socialism would mean the end of all bloodshed. She was prepared to take on that responsibility.

3.8. Scherl Publishing House
former Scherl-Verlag — Axel-Springer-Passage —
Zimmerstraße 28-32

When the revolution reached Berlin on November 9, 1918, Rosa
Luxemburg was still stuck in Breslau. She had been released from
the fortress prison the previous day, but trains were only going
to Frankfurt (Oder). She managed to squeeze into a train on
November 10, sitting on top of her suitcase in the aisle, hoping
that none of the soldiers would recognize her. That train unex-
pectedly continued to Berlin, stopping at Schlesischer Bahnhof
(which is now Ostbahnhof). Liebknecht had been welcomed
back to Berlin three weeks earlier by thousands of cheering proletarians. (See Stop 2.5) Luxemburg, in contrast, arrived at 10pm
on a chilly night, with only a few close friends to greet her. Three
years in prison had made her hair turn white. But despite her
weakness, she threw herself into the revolution she had been preparing for decades.

The previous night, as the dust was settling after the insurrection, Spartacists had gone to one of Berlin's biggest publishing
houses, the Scherl-Verlag. The imposing building towered above
Zimmerstraße, occupying most of the block between Jerusalemer
Straße and Markgrafenstraße. A viciously reactionary tabloid,
the *Berliner Lokalanzeiger*, was published here.

Hermann Duncker, Ernst Meyer, and other Spartacists, accompanied by a few revolutionary soldiers, took over the building
without encountering resistance. Duncker gathered all the journalists and printers together to let them know they would now
be publishing a revolutionary newspaper. "You understand," he

said, "that a victorious revolution cannot tolerate a counterrevolutionary press." Socialist revolutions use such direct language!

The first issue of *Die Rote Fahne* appeared with a banner headline: "Berlin under the red flag." But as the revolutionaries had only arrived in the evening, most of the issue consisted of articles that had been written previously by capitalist journalists. The second issue, completed on the evening of November 10, was more consistent. By this time, however, the editors were recovering their courage. Friedrich Ebert, who was claiming to be chancellor, had ordered that the paper be handed back to its former owners. Richard Müller from the workers' council counter-ordered that it now belonged to the Spartacists. Arriving on the evening of November 10, Luxemburg gave a passionate speech that convinced the printers to complete the second issue. Soon, however, drunken soldiers sent by the government came and detained the Spartacists.

They moved to the Hotel Excelsior at Königgrätzer Straße 112-113, opposite Anhalter Bahnhof. This was among the largest hotels in Europe. Today that spot is occupied by an office and apartment building at Stresemanstraße 78 called the Excelsior-haus. This was Luxemburg's home for the next few days — and this is where the Spartacus Group was transformed into the Spartacus League at a conference on November 11.

It took a week before the Spartacists were able to find a new printer for their daily. A bourgeois paper called *Das kleine Journal*, located at Königgrätzer Straße 40-41, agreed to publish *Die Rote Fahne*. Today a brand new office building belonging to Germany's environmental ministry stands there, at Stresemanstraße 69. The Spartacists' central office was set up in a hotel at

Wilhelmstraße 114, but they had to move around the block to Friedrichstraße 217 after just a few days. This area is where Luxemburg spent most of the final 68 days of her life.

Luxemburg became a terrifying figure for all the forces of reaction. General Georg Maercker said at the time: "This Rosa Luxemburg is a she-devil ... Rosa Luxemburg could destroy the German Reich today and not be touched. There is no force in the Reich that is capable of opposing her."

It's amazing to think about: Luxemburg was a woman in a society that completely excluded women from political life. She was an immigrant who spoke German with an accent, and she was Jewish. She was 1.5 meters (five feet) tall and she walked with a limp. Yet for the most powerful men in the German Empire, she represented an unstoppable force — because she was speaking for millions of workers who wanted radical change.

Today, the Scherl-Verlag has been replaced by the Axel-Springer-Verlag. The modern version of the *Lokal-Anzeiger*, the reactionary tabloids *Bild* and *B.Z.*, are produced in fancy new buildings covering the same block. Almost exactly 50 years after the events described here, radicals again tried to occupy the publishing house, calling for the expropriation of Springer. (See Stop 5.9)

3.9. *Alfred Bernstein*
Blücherstraße 13

Blücherstraße is a busy thoroughfare through Kreuzberg. The big streets in this part of Kreuzberg are named after mostly forgotten Prussian generals: Walking through Yorckstraße,

Gneisenaustraße, or Blücherstraße, no one will think of Ludwig Graf Yorck von Wartenburg, August Neidhardt von Gneisenau, or Leberecht von Blücher. These were the heroes of what Germans used to call their "liberation wars." These generals pushed back Napoleon, and thus saved absolutism in Europe for another century. Very slowly, a discussion about changing these names is underway.

Blücherstraße 13, opposite the Holy Cross Church, is where Luxemburg and Liebknecht went into hiding on January 10, 1919. After the January Uprising was defeated (see Stop 2.10), their friends urged them to go underground. Big capitalists had sponsored red posters hanging all over the city: "Beat the leaders [of the Spartacus Group] to death! Kill Liebknecht!"

Their first hiding place, however, was not far from the fighting. In fact, it was just half a kilometer from the battle at the *Vorwärts* building. The Freikorps began their attack in the evening of November 10 — Luxemburg and Liebknecht would have heard the artillery and seen the smoke. The next morning, the occupiers were forced to surrender. Neither side would have realized the leaders of the revolution were a short walk away.

This first hiding place was far from anonymous. It was the home of Dr. Alfred Bernstein, an anarcho-socialist doctor and a member of Kreuzberg's local council. Bernstein is remembered for two things: Firstly, he was one of the founders of the Workers Samaritan League (ASB) which offered first aid courses. Secondly, Bernstein was an advocate of the "birth strike." At the time, it was primarily socialists and anarchists who were spreading information about birth control. Bernstein and his co-thinkers went a step further: They said birth control could be employed as a means of political struggle.

"The decline in the birth rate is striking capitalism in its marrow" Bernstein declared at an overflowing assembly of 2,000 women workers on August 22, 1913. "If we don't recruit new objects of exploitation, if we don't grow the army, then capitalism is finished." The meeting in the Neue Welt (New World) at Hasenheide 107 had been called by the SPD Berlin. The party brought its most prominent women to oppose Bernstein's idea. Clara Zetkin reminded the audience that throughout history, an oppressed class could only liberate itself with overwhelming numbers. For her, a decline in the birth rate would reduce the number of "soldiers for the revolution." Luxemburg, too, said the proletariat needed as many babies as possible.

Zetkin and Luxemburg were not able to convince the assembly to oppose birth control — the prepared resolution against the birth strike was not passed. Luise Zeitz, another leading social democrat, soon declared that birth control was a private decision. More and more socialists started demanding that women have control over their own bodies. (At the same time, it should be mentioned that Bernstein, along with other early advocates of birth control such as Margaret Singer in New York City, held deeply troubling eugenicist views.) By 1920, it was socialist women from the USPD and the KPD who were leading the campaign to abolish paragraph 218 of Germany's criminal code, which prohibits abortion. (See Stop 9.5)

Less than five years after their showdown over birth control, Bernstein offered refuge to Luxemburg and Liebknecht. But the next day, his maid began talking about the prominent guests. So after two nights, they had to flee to the apartment of a working-class family in Neukölln. (See Stop 4.14) Here, they held meetings around the clock — Rosa Luxemburg, for example, gave instructions to Hugo Eberlein as he was leaving for Moscow as the KPD's delegate to the founding congress of the Communist International. The host family became nervous about all the people coming and going, and after two more days, on January 14, Luxemburg and Liebknecht moved to a more tranquil area.

3.10. Siegfried Marcusson
Mannheimer Straße 27 (formerly 43)

The district of Wilmersdorf has been fused with Charlottenburg and shares the same characteristics: What was once a refuge for the lower and middle bourgeoisie is now more or less a retirement community. The white building with an elegant entrance was the home of Siegfried and Wanda Marcusson — the latter had worked in the Soviet embassy and was a friend of Luxemburg's. Their apartment was on the first floor, and including the window above the main entrance. Luxemburg and Liebknecht arrived here on January 14, 1919. Against the advice of their friends, they insisted on staying together to maintain some kind of leadership for the revolution.

The insurrection of January 1919 is even today referred to as the "Spartacist Uprising." But it is clear that actual Spartacists, i.e. members of the Communist Party, played a relatively minor role. Liebknecht had pressed forward as part of the Revolution Committee, but Luxemburg was more hesitant, as she understood that the revolution needed more time to gather its forces before the final battle.

In Wilmersdorf, Rosa Luxemburg completed what would become her final article. She quoted a song by Ferdinand Freiligrath about the failed revolution in 1848, as this new revolution had also suffered a defeat. The bourgeois press was celebrating the restoration of order. Luxemburg retorted:

'Order prevails in Berlin!' You foolish lackeys! Your 'order' is built on sand. Tomorrow the revolution will 'rise up again, clashing its weapons,' and to your horror it will proclaim with trumpets blazing: I was, I am, I shall be!

The following evening, the Marcussons' apartment was searched by a Bürgerwehr, a self-proclaimed "citizens' militia." Soldiers armed with steel helmets, rifles, and grenades had gotten a tip from government spies tapping the telephone lines. Luxemburg did not try to hide her identity. She had already been arrested so many times — she quickly packed her favorite books for passing the time in prison. Liebknecht was taken to a school where the right-wing vigilantes had their headquarters — the former girls' school is now the Cecilien-Grundschule (Nikolsburger Platz 5). Both were then handed over to a Freikorps under the command of Waldemar Pabst.

What would happen to these two famous prisoners? In retrospect, the end of this story seems inevitable. We are left to wonder why Luxemburg and Liebknecht did not attempt to flee to Hamburg, Jena, or Switzerland until reaction subsided. But Luxemburg had been in the prisons of the Russian Tsar and the

German Kaiser — neither had considered simply murdering her. Even these autocrats felt it was important to maintain some semblance of justice.

When workers in Petrograd carried out a premature uprising in July 1917, the government tried to crush the revolutionary movement. Lenin did go into hiding — but Trotsky surrendered to the authorities and was put in prison. Again, no one contemplated shooting the leader of the soviet. Trotsky spent two months in prison and, as he had confidently expected, was liberated by the next wave of the revolution.

How could Luxemburg, or anyone else, have imagined that a social democratic government would be willing to commit a crime too heinous for the Tsar or the Kaiser? This was not just any social democratic government — just a decade earlier, Ebert had been Luxemburg's student. Yet Ebert was willing to cross that line, and the horrific crime would not remain an isolated transgression against the rules of civilization: As one historian put it, Mannheimer Straße leads straight to Dachau and Buchenwald.

3.11. Eden Hotel
Olof-Palme-Platz

This small square surrounds a fountain made of 100 tons of ancient rocks. It serves as a portal to the Berlin Aquarium, next to the Elephant Gate of the Berlin Zoo. There was not always a square here — Budapester Straße once ran right in front of the Aquarium. On the other side of the street, a triangular block contained one of Berlin's swankiest hotels, the Eden Hotel (not to be confused with a much less fancy establishment bearing the same name today).

In early 1919, Budapester Straße was blocked off with barbed wire. The hotel was the headquarters of the Guards Cavalry Rifle Division (GKSD), a military unit under the command of Captain Waldemar Pabst. Liebknecht and Luxemburg were delivered here at 9:30 and 10 p.m. After several hours of interrogations, Pabst was uncertain about what to do with his prisoners. The idea of an assassination was in the air — the posters were everywhere — but would Pabst dare to give the order?

He called the Reich Chancellery and reached war minister Gustav Noske. Ebert was in the room and listening. Noske told Pabst to give the order himself. Pabst refused. Noske suggested asking Reinhardt, another Freikorps commander, but Pabst was certain that Reinhardt would give the same answer. This went back and forth, until Noske declared: "Then you have to know yourself what has to be done."

Pabst and his friends worked out a plan to commit murder without anyone taking responsibility. They finally led Liebknecht and Luxemburg out of the hotel. Liebknecht was hit on the head with a rifle butt and placed in a car, supposedly to be taken to the prison in Moabit. In the Tiergarten, the driver claimed the car had broken down. Liebknecht got out and was promptly shot in the back, supposedly "while attempting to escape." This became the preferred method for German police to dispose of revolutionaries — in the following years, countless leaders were murdered "while attempting to escape."

The Berlin Aquarium, by the way, opened in 1913. I have not found any evidence that Luxemburg ever visited. But it is hard to imagine she could resist the opportunity to see live crocodiles and other magical creatures. In a letter from the countryside in 1904, she reported encountering "all kinds of animals that I've otherwise only seen through bars in the zoo." She could almost picture herself running into "a leopard, rhinos, and aurochses."

3.12. A Corpse in the Canal
Landwehrkanal, under the Lichtenstein Bridge

Luxemburg was led out of the hotel separately, and as soon as she reached the sidewalk, the same soldier struck her on the head twice with the butt of his rifle. Her unconscious body was packed into a car and here a different soldier shot her in the head. The car also headed toward the Tiergarten. Luxemburg's corpse was thrown off the Lichtenstein Bridge into the canal. The murderers claimed that an angry mob had dragged Luxemburg off, and they had no idea where she was.

It was only on May 31, four and a half months later, that a female corpse was dragged out of the Landwehrkanal. A few weeks earlier, a military tribunal of the GKSD had handed down a light sentence to one soldier for "attempted murder" — despite the fact that everyone knew the "attempt" had been successful. In other words, commanders were passing judgement on the soldiers who had carried out their orders. One of these commanders then helped the condemned soldier flee the country. Pabst was never even charged. He went on to have a successful career under the Nazis and an even more successful career in West Germany, protected by the secret services. At the end of his life, he put his discussions with Noske and Ebert on the record.

Have the social democrats ever accepted their responsibility for the most nefarious political assassination of the twentieth century (with apologies to Leon Trotsky and Mahatma Gandhi)? No. When the centenary of the murder arrived in 2018, SPD leaders wondered out loud: Who can really know who gave the order? Can the account of a proto-fascist like Pabst be trusted?

It's true that there is no written order from Noske to murder Luxemburg and Liebknecht. He did, however, write that Freikorps should shoot so-called "Spartacists" on sight. (See Stop 2.11) Is it conceivable that Noske would have stopped short of killing the leading Spartacists? The evidence, as compiled by Klaus Gietinger and many other historians, is overwhelming, even though no German court has ever looked at it seriously.

The Lichtenstein Bridge is today divided into two pedestrian bridges, separated by spikes. One connects the two parts of the Berlin Zoo, the other belongs to the Tiergarten. Underneath the bridge, a metal sculpture with Luxemburg's name rises out of the water. She probably would have enjoyed the fact that she is commemorated just a few meters from the enclosure of a creature as improbable as the giant anteater. Beside the New Lake, 200 meters to the north, a brick column marks the spot where Liebknecht was shot.

3.13. Memorial of the Socialists
Gedenkstätte der Sozialisten — Gudrunstraße 20

Liebknecht was buried in the Central Cemetery of Friedrichsfelde far in the East. This had once been Berlin's "poor people's cemetery." After prominent socialists like Wilhelm Liebknecht chose to be buried here as well, it became the "socialists' cemetery."

Liebknecht and Luxemburg were supposed to be interred in the Cemetery of the March Fallen at Ernst-Zinna-Weg 1 in Volkspark Friedrichshain. This is where Berlin's working class remembered the heroes who died on the barricades of March 1848. When a new revolution arrived in 1918, this cemetery was quickly expanded. On November 20, 1918, Erich Habersaath and seven more workers who died during the Berlin uprising were buried here. Further soldiers and sailors who were murdered by the counterrevolution were put to rest on December 20 and December 29. Yet the SPD refused to allow the dead from the January Uprising to be included.

This is how the two communist leaders ended up in Friedrichsfelde. After a funeral procession of 100,000 people, Liebknecht was lowered into the ground on January 25. An empty casket for Rosa Luxemburg was buried alongside his. Luxemburg's body was added at another massive funeral on June 13.

In 1926, the Communist Party unveiled a Revolution Monument for its two founders. The modernist brick construction, designed by Ludwig Mies van der Rohe, contained a red star with a hammer and sickle as well as Luxemburg's final words: "I was, I am, I shall be." The graves were destroyed by the Nazis in 1935, with the star preserved for a time in a Nazi museum at Taubenstraße 7 (the "Revolution Museum of SA Standard 6").

The East German government built a new monument, the Memorial of the Socialists, in 1951. As the Socialist Unity Party (SED) claimed the traditions of both the Social Democratic Party and the Communist Party, this monument combines graves of SPD and KPD leaders. Older gravestones from the cemetery were collected here and set up alongside newer ones. A giant stone reminds visitors: "The dead warn us." In 1958, the Cemetery of the March Fallen was remodeled for the 110th and 40th anniversaries of the two revolutions, with a bronze statue dedicated to the Red Sailor.

Every year since 1919, there have been Luxemburg-Liebknecht demonstrations on the second Sunday in January — since 1924 these have been expanded into Luxemburg-Liebknecht-Lenin demonstrations. They start at Frankfurter Tor and end at the cemetery gates. Even today, up to 100,000 people leave red carnations for socialists who could not be killed.

The German state spends tens of millions of euros a year to turn Luxemburg into a "harmless icon." This is done via a reformist foundation run by — to use Luxemburg's disdainful term — "government socialists." The revolutionary communist is presented as a democrat and a pacifist who would have supported the modern capitalist regime.

Luxemburg was certainly no fan of violence for its own sake — but she had just witnessed Europe's ruling classes slaughter ten million people in order to prop up their tottering system. She was not so naive as to think that the capitalists would relinquish power if they were asked nicely. Not long before her death, she declared: "Socialism does not mean sitting down in a parliament and passing laws. Socialism for us means toppling the ruling classes with the full brutality that the proletariat can develop in its struggle." A few weeks earlier, she said: "Whoever opposes the armored car of socialist revolution will end up lying on the ground with broken limbs."

A year and a half before her death, Luxemburg wrote to Sophie Liebknecht: "I will ... hopefully die at my post: in a street battle or in prison." And she did. While she was unable to lead the German Revolution to its conclusion, she provided an example that inspires revolutionaries today. Her legacy is best summed up in a single quote: "The revolution is magnificent. Everything else is nonsense."

Workers and soldiers outside the Neukölln City Hall in December 1918.
The banner reads, "Proletarians of all countries, unite!" See Stops 4.2
and 4.4. Photographer unknown. Via Wikimedia Commons.

4

Neukölln Will Stay Red

4.1. Richard Square
Richardplatz

In popular media, Neukölln is made to look like Berlin's version of South Central Los Angeles. TV series like *4 Blocks* and *Dogs of Berlin* show a neighborhood in the grip of "criminal clans."

In reality, Neukölln is *Multikulti* at its best and at its worst. Neukölln is people from more than 100 nations living together. The "Avenue of the Sun," the Sonnenallee, is a center of Arab culture in Germany. But Neukölln is also generations of state racism, poverty, and everything that implies. Neukölln has been my home for more than a decade as well.

About half of the district's 330,000 residents "have a migration background after 1945," which is the way the bureaucracy says "not ethnic German." The unemployment rate, at 16%, is the highest in the city. During the wave of the Covid-19 pandemic, there were twice as many cases in Neukölln as in wealthier neighborhoods. Racist politicians said this was because all the "Ausländer" (foreigners) were not following the rules. The simple truth is that the population density here is more than double what it is in Zehlendorf.

Historically, Neukölln was a communist stronghold — the reddest of Berlin's red districts. In the last elections of the Weimar

Republic, in November 1932, the Communist Party of Germany (KPD) got 39.3% of the votes here. The Social Democratic Party (SPD) got another 26.2%. So almost two thirds of Neuköllners voted for the two workers' parties. The Nazis, in contrast, got just 22.2%.

In March 1933, after Hitler was already in power, the Nazis held rigged elections. The KPD had been prohibited and its leaders were in prison — the party had to campaign as "List 3." Even so, the communists remained Neukölln's biggest party, with 32% of votes!

People like to claim that Hitler came to power by winning elections. In reality, however, he was named Reich Chancellor by a bourgeois politician, and formed a minority government in coalition with bourgeois parties. Hitler never won a majority of votes — and his so-called "workers' party" never even came close in workers' districts like Neukölln.

If you struggle through this bustling, overcrowded neighborhood, pushing toward the center, you will end up in… a village. Richardplatz is a picturesque square made of ancient cobblestones, with a round kiosk on one side and a working blacksmith's on the other. There are farmhouses and barns (some of which have been converted into hipster bars), as well as stables full of horses. This is the center of old Rixdorf. This hamlet, now surrounded by high-rises, is the heart of Neukölln.

Rixdorf was founded in 1737 by refugees from Bohemia. They were Protestants, and after their homeland was forcibly converted to Catholicism, the Prussian King Friedrich Wilhelm I allowed them to settle here and practice their religion. In thanks, they put up a statue of the Soldier King just north of this square in Kirchgasse.

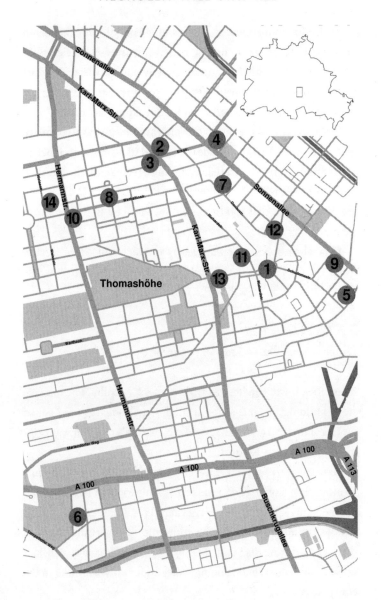

As Berlin industrialized toward the end of the nineteenth century, Rixdorf grew into a massive workers' district right outside the city. With over 200,000 mostly poor residents, Rixdorf had a reputation for dance halls, bars, prostitution, and generally poor morals. A popular ballad said: "In Rixdorf ist Musike."

City elders were prepared to take drastic measures to improve that reputation. In 1912, Rixdorf changed its name. A number of alternatives were considered, including Hermannstadt, but they settled on Neukölln — a reference to Cölln, a small village on the Spree Island that had been swallowed up by Berlin centuries earlier.

This whole maneuver was clearly unsuccessful. Here we are, more than a century later, and Neukölln's reputation is worse than ever. Maybe they should rename it again?

4.2. *Rixdorf City Hall*
Rathaus Neukölln — Karl-Marx-Straße 83

This clock tower can be seen from across Neukölln. The massive stone building, in an L-shape around a small square, was opened on December 8, 1908. What is now Neukölln's city hall was originally the Rathaus Rixdorf.

Between 1871 and 1910, the city grew from 8,000 inhabitants to more than a quarter of a million. Most people in Rixdorf lived in tenements known as Mietskasernen (literally: rental barracks). Whole families would share an entire room — often renting out their beds during the day. There was little light and constant noise, while toilets and running water could only be found in the courtyards.

The Social Democratic Party (SPD), which at the time still considered itself a revolutionary Marxist party, was strong in proletarian Rixdorf. The SPD won the most votes in municipal elections — but this did not translate into the most seats on the city council. Prussia had a "three-class franchise system," meaning that the people who paid the top third of tax revenue got one third of seats, while the other thirds were similarly distributed. When the system was introduced in 1849, the first class made up just 5% of the population, and the third class 83%. In some districts, the entire first class consisted of a single capitalist, who thus picked his own personal representative in parliament. A bourgeois member of the Rixdorf city council explained the logic: "If you have big responsibilities in the city, you should be given the corresponding rights."

The SPD won every single seat for the city's third class, and by 1908, three seats for the second class as well. The bourgeois parties were getting nervous that the majority might soon be able to exercise power.

The first time the city council met in their new building was on December 17, 1908. The bourgeois majority wanted to change the election law, increasing the tax threshold for the first and second classes. Workers came out to protest against this "theft of voting rights." They filled the galleries above the council. They packed the hallways and stairwells as well, spilling out onto the street — 15,000 workers in total.

The bourgeois press called this "red terror." In reality, the protest was completely peaceful — organized workers in Germany tended to be law-abiding and well-behaved. Police ordered the workers to disperse, and they did. The bourgeois councilors then passed their reform.

The "Rixdorf theft of voting rights" made news across Germany. The Kaiser had been talking about "modernizing" the three-class franchise system. The German workers' movement had always demanded equal voting rights — in the words of Ferdinand Lasalle, this was the "workers' principle slogan and banner," and the "lever" for winning all other rights. There were a few voices on the SPD's right wing who wanted to negotiate with the Kaiser. But the example in Rixdorf proved that any so-called "reform" was just going to make things less democratic. The demand remained: Equal voting rights for all!

This ended up being a moot point. No reform ever happened — just ten years later, the revolution of 1918 brought equal voting rights all at once.

4.3. Fritz Haberland
Neckarstraße 3

Opposite the city hall and just a few meters up the hill, we will reach an unassuming yellow apartment building. The ground floor is occupied by a tailor's and a store for plumbing fixtures. Hardly a place you would expect to find a hive of revolutionary activity — but when the SPD collapsed, this is where the seeds of a new party for Neukölln's working class were planted.

The SPD had always been an anti-war party. But when World War I broke out in 1914, the leadership threw their support behind the Kaiser. They expelled the party's revolutionary left wing (including Rosa Luxemburg and Karl Liebknecht) but also the lukewarm pacifists from the center (such as Karl Kautsky). In 1917, all the people expelled from the SPD founded the Independent Social Democratic Party of Germany (USPD). The USPD included the Spartacus League, the organization of the radical left. (See Stop 2.4)

Spartacus was a tiny group: Its most prominent leaders spent the war in prison, and its few hundred members were subject to constant repression. It was only once the revolution began that they could build a real organization. On December 12, 1918, Fritz Haberland set up an office for the group's Neukölln district here at Neckarstraße 3.

A few weeks earlier, on November 21, Luxemburg had spoken to a mass meeting just down the road. She was greeted by thunderous applause in the Passage Festsäle. That hall still exists today at Karl-Marx-Straße 131, home to the Neukölln Oper and the Passage Kino cinema. She declared that the revolution's biggest mistake had been leaving all the state officials in their positions.

As 1918 came to a close, the Spartacists decided to leave the USPD to launch their own party: The Communist Party of Germany. Few joined the split, however. The USPD remained a mass party with hundreds of thousands of members, while the KPD started as a sect with a tiny fraction of that.

Except in Neukölln! On December 30, 1918, the USPD of Neukölln held a general assembly. It took place in a hall at the Union Brewery on Hasenheide. The breweries and beer halls that once lined the street are mostly gone (except for the Neue Welt). They served as important meeting places for social democracy, which encouraged workers to abandon schnapps and instead drink beer.

Up to 3,000 USPD members showed up for a rhetorical duel between some of the biggest names of the international socialist movement. Karl Liebknecht was arguing for a new revolutionary party. The defense of the USPD was taken up by its chairman Hugo Haase, who just days earlier had resigned from the German government. He got international support from the head of the new Austrian government, state chancellor Karl Renner. Clearly, both sides pulled out all the stops to win the loyalty of Neukölln's working class.

After hours of debate, the assembly voted: 2,900 were in favor of the new communist party, and just 100 wanted to stick with the old USPD. That same day, the KPD's founding congress opened. (See Stop 2.9) Neukölln was thus a communist stronghold before the communist party even existed.

4.4. Rixdorf Police Presidium
Polizeiabschnitt 54 — Sonnenallee 107

This fortress made out of red brick and stone dominates Sonnenallee. The tower at the very top is missing, but aside from that, it looks almost exactly like it did when it opened in 1902. This was once the Royal Police Presidium of Rixdorf — now it is the 54th precinct of the Berlin Police. The Kiez has changed almost beyond recognition, but this building is the same, telling everyone: Germany's political regimes might come and go, but the police are eternal.

When the revolution reached Berlin and the surrounding cities on November 9, 1918, Neukölln workers understood that they needed to neutralize the cops. On the morning of the general strike, a local Spartacist named Willy Willies led a crowd of workers through the Neukölln streets. They stopped in front of schools, which had been commandeered by the military for use as barracks, and called on the young soldiers to join the uprising.

Thousands of demonstrators then marched to this police station. The cops barricaded themselves inside. Surrounded by an angry mob with plenty of rifles, they did not offer any resistance. Instead, they admitted a delegation led by Willies, who later recalled:

> In our negotiations with the chief of police, we demanded that the police guards immediately lay down their arms, that we be allowed to visit political prisoners as well as those accused of minor crimes. Given the situation, he had no choice but to fulfill our demands. ... We released a number of political prisoners, as well as some arrested for crimes committed out of poverty, including a boy who stole bread.

The police were allowed to leave, abandoning their weapons and uniforms. They were prohibited from ever working as police again (a "Berufsverbot"). One police officer recalled this as "the most shameful hour of my life."

The revolutionaries continued to the city hall just a block away. A workers' and soldiers' council of Neukölln was quickly elected, with Fritz Haberland as chair. They raised the red flag over the clock tower, and a banner over the entrance proclaimed: "Proletarians of all countries, unite!"

The new government's first proclamation, titled *Weltrevolution*, called for the "disarming of all police" and the "arming of the people," as well as the "expropriation of the capitalists" and the "abolition of private property." These lofty goals were combined with practical measures as well. On December 2, all rent increases and evictions were banned: "Any exploitation of the working or unemployed population is prohibited!" A measure that Neukölln could desperately use today!

On December 12, the workers' council dissolved the old city council, as it had been elected undemocratically. The "Republic of Neukölln" struck fear in the hearts of the German bourgeoisie. The national government, under the social democrat Friedrich Ebert, sent troops to occupy the city and arrest the workers' council. These Freikorps reinstalled the old local government on December 19.

4.5. Leo Jogiches
Schwarzastraße 9

This pink apartment building, overlooking a small square opposite the S-Bahn station Sonnenallee, was clearly built for the finer residents of a proletarian neighborhood. More than a century later, it fulfills the same role, housing trendy eateries that stand out among the area's Spätis.

This was the home of Berlin's most important communist you've probably never heard of. The founding chairpersons of the KPD, Rosa Luxemburg and Karl Liebknecht, were assassinated on January 15, 1919. They were known to workers around the world. Their replacement was a shadow.

Leo Jogiches has been called the "man behind Rosa Luxemburg." She was a passionate speaker and writer — he, in contrast, liked neither speaking nor writing. As Luxemburg said: "The mere thought of putting his ideas on paper paralyzes him." Jogiches was an organizer behind the scenes.

Jogiches had been born into a wealthy Jewish family in Vilnius, then part of the Tsarist Empire, in 1867. He joined the socialist movement at 18, and soon went into exile in Switzerland. There he met Rosa Luxemburg, three years his junior, and they founded a Polish socialist newspaper and then an organization: the Social Democracy of the Kingdom of Poland and Lithuania (SDKPiL).

Luxemburg moved to Berlin in 1898 to be near the center of the international socialist movement — at just 27, she soon became a leading voice in the SPD's debates. Jogiches soon followed but kept out of view. Their relationship ended around 1907, but they remained comrades-in-arms.

Not long after World War I began, Luxemburg was thrown into prison for an anti-war speech she had given in 1913. (See Stop 3.6) From her cell, she wrote articles against the war. Jogiches was the one who made sure these texts were smuggled out of the jail, printed in illegal workshops, and distributed to workers across Germany. The underground publication was titled *Spartacus* — and the underground network led by Jogiches was soon known as the Spartacus Group. Unlike most other leading Spartacists, Jogiches evaded arrest until early 1918. He was freed by the revolution, on the same day as Luxemburg.

After the assassination of Luxemburg and Liebknecht, Jogiches remained at his post at the head of the KPD. He worked at the editorial office near Anhalter Bahnhof and took the S-Bahn back home to Neukölln every night. He directed the newspaper *Die Rote Fahne* while still writing very little. Paul Frölich, the youngest member of the KPD's leadership, described him thus: "Leo was a dictator who always remained in the shadows. Only a very few people knew him. And beyond the narrow circle of his collaborators, only a few knew of his very existence." Jogiches investigated the murders, and within a month had published names and photos of the killers — that is more than any German court has done to this day!

His friends urged him to go underground — his predecessors had just been murdered by proto-fascist paramilitaries, after all. But with Luxemburg's death, Jogiches seems to have lost the will to live. This master of conspiracy said he couldn't leave his official address because that would be an imposition on his landlady. It almost seems like suicide by cop. On March 10, 1919, the police came for him. Jogiches was taken to the jail in Moabit, and that same day, a police officer named Ernst Tamschick shot him in the back of the head ("while attempting to escape," of course). Tamschick was never even put on trial.

4.6. Ruth Fischer
Andreasberger Straße 9

At first glance, this white building with brick trim might appear to be an uninspired post-war housing project. But it is actually a design from 1926 in the Bauhaus style. Around the corner, the complex presents its full glory with a pedestrian walkway where each doorway has a unique brickwork pattern.

This was the home of Ruth Fischer. In 1924, Fischer was elected head of the Communist Party's Zentrale — at just 28, she led a party with hundreds of thousands of members. The KPD was the first German party headed by a woman, with Rosa Luxemburg — and also the second, with Ruth Fischer.

Born in Vienna as Elfriede Eisler, Fischer was a passionate speaker in the Reichstag and at mass rallies. As the main leader of the KPD's ultraleft wing, she was skeptical of any kind of united front with social democrats. In 1926, she was expelled by the party's new Stalinist leadership. She then got a job as a social worker — that is when she moved into this building.

As a prominent Bolshevik and a Jew, she was at the very top of the Nazis' enemies list. Her apartment was ransacked by stormtroopers just a few days after Hitler established his dictatorship. She fled into exile and became the first woman to have her German citizenship revoked.

Fischer ended up in the United States, and eventually testified for McCarthy's House Un-American Activities Committee, denouncing her brother Gerhart Eisler as a Soviet agent. Another brother, Hanns Eisler, was a composer and collaborator of Bertolt Brecht. From 1955 until her death in 1961, Fischer lived in Paris and worked as a leftist journalist. In February 2022, I got commemorative brass cobblestones (Stolpersteine) placed for Fischer, her partner, and her son at this address.

4.7. *Olga Benario*
Innstraße 24

There were many communists in Neukölln. But only one became so famous that a feature film was made about them in Brazil in 2004. They lived in this unassuming grey-blue building at the corner of Innstraße and Donaustraße.

Olga Benario was born in 1908 as the daughter of a prominent social democratic lawyer in Munich. At age 15, in a perfect act of teenage rebellion, she joined the Communist Youth League (KJVD). At 18, she moved to Neukölln, as many people considered Berlin to be the center of the world revolution. A charismatic speaker and talented organizer, Benario was soon the leader of Neukölln's young communists.

In October 1926, her boyfriend Otto Braun was arrested on charges of spying for the Soviet Union. Benario was thrown in prison as well, but after two months, her father managed to secure her release. On April 11, 1928, she went to visit Braun in the Moabit jail. Half a dozen more young communists from Neukölln forced their way into the visitation room. They drew pistols, held the guards at bay, and swept the couple into a getaway car — a spectacular coup by the KPD's secret service, the *M-Apparat*.

Within days, wanted posters all over the city were offering 5,000 Reichsmark for Braun and Benario (as much as a worker would earn in several years). The story was already vaguely romantic, but when rumors spread that the pistols hadn't even been loaded, the working class decided they loved the 20-year-old folk hero. (The police did themselves no favors by publishing pictures of her in an awesome black leather jacket.) She escaped to Czechoslovakia and continued on to Moscow. There, she began working in the leadership of the Communist Youth International and trained with the Red Army, learning to shoot a machine gun, ride a horse, and parachute out of an airplane. Secret missions took her to different European countries.

At the time, a famous guest was staying in Moscow. Luís Carlos Prestes, a former officer of the Brazilian military, had led a guerrilla army across that enormous country. This Prestes Column fought against the landed oligarchy. It was eventually defeated, but its leader was remembered as a Brazilian Zapata. Prestes went to the Soviet Union for three years. In 1934, he returned to Brazil to found a popular front and launch an insurrection against the dictatorship.

Olga Benario was assigned to serve as Prestes's advisor and bodyguard, and before they arrived in Brazil the two were also a couple. The attempted uprising in late 1935, however, was a fiasco, and numerous communists were arrested.

The Brazilian government wanted to deport Benario, a Jewish communist, to Nazi Germany. The Supreme Court had to answer an interesting question. Benario was pregnant. Her future child would be a Brazilian citizen, and Brazil could not deport its nationals. So how did this deeply Catholic court rule? It declared that the fetus was not a person! Benario was deported back to Berlin and ended up in the women's prison on Barnim-straße — the same place where Rosa Luxemburg had been held 20 years earlier. (See Stop 3.6) Her jailers noted that Benario was an "extremely dangerous prisoner." She was sent to a concentration camp and in 1942 was gassed alongside hundreds of other women.

Benario gave birth to a daughter in prison, and the girl was saved by her Brazilian grandmother. A Stolperstein was placed in front of Benario's apartment on the 100th anniversary of her birth in 2008. Her daughter, the Brazilian historian Anita Prestes, was present for the ceremony. A few blocks away, a Galerie Olga Benario in Richardstraße 104 carries on her antifascist legacy.

4.8. Communist Youth International
Parking lot of the Rewe supermarket at Rollbergstraße 59
(formerly back room of a bar at Ziethenstraße 29)

For this stop, we have to stand in the parking lot in front of the
Rewe supermarket at Rollbergstraße 59. Not only have the street
names and the house numbers changed — the entire kiez is gone.
The Rollbergviertel around the old Kindl brewery was once
packed with tenements. In the 1970s, these were torn down and
replaced with massive housing projects. This parking lot used to
be Ziethenstraße 29 (which is today Werbellinstraße), and we
can imagine standing in the back room of a bar on the ground
floor.

On November 20, 1919, a pigeon breeders' association met
in this "dark, dirty, small back room." Strangely, the pigeon
breeders were all under 25, and had come from 14 countries
across Europe, including Russia. This was in fact the founding
congress of the Communist Youth International, which met in
strict secrecy — in 1919, Germany's social democratic government still had the city under martial law. Each day, the delegates
gathered at a different location, including the studio of the revolutionary artist Käthe Kollwitz (see Stop 9.4) and the Sanssouci
palace in Potsdam. After six days, the CYI was born.

The leader of this meeting was Willi Münzenberg, who had once
been a young worker from Erfurt. He set off wandering through
Germany and ended up in Zurich. There, he became active in
the Swiss socialist youth movement. When World War I broke
out and the Socialist Youth International collapsed, Münzenberg
— based in a neutral country — took the lead in coordinating

anti-war socialists across Europe. Working together with V.I. Lenin and other exiles in Zurich, he became more radical. He published a magazine called *Jugend-Internationale* and led the preparations to re-found the youth international.

The CYI was no mere front for the Communist International. During World War I, the socialist youth organizations had rebelled against their parent parties. The parties generally supported the war, while the youth organizations began protesting against it. As the war ended and a revolutionary period began, many youth organizations broke off on their own, and they were not inclined to submit to any adult party, not even a communist one. Therefore, the new youth international declared itself independent and only "organizationally connected" to the Comintern. Until 1921, its international headquarters was in Berlin, hidden in a basement in Schöneberg, to keep it autonomous from the Comintern apparatus in Moscow.

By the mid-1920s, the youth international had been brought under the control of the Stalinists, who dissolved it in 1943. But it was started in Neukölln.

4.9. *Anton Grylewicz*
Brusendorfer Straße 23

In the early 1930s, Leon Trotsky, trapped in exile on the Turkish island of Prinkipo, wrote a series of pamphlets warning the German workers' movement about the threat of fascism. Perry Anderson has called these works "the first real Marxist analysis of a twentieth century capitalist state" and "unmatched in the field of historical materialism." Over 67,000 copies of Trotsky's pamphlets were published in 1932 in Germany — at an address currently occupied by a particularly ugly house from the 1950s with concrete-and-brick balconies.

This was once the home of metal worker Anton Grylewicz. During World War I, Grylewicz joined a secret group of trade unionists who became known as the Revolutionary Stewards. They organized strikes against the war, including the general strike on November 9, 1918. Grylewicz then became the deputy to Emil Eichhorn, Berlin's revolutionary police chief. (See Stops 2.1. and 2.10) In the Communist Party, Grylewicz worked as an organizer for Ruth Fischer's ultraleft wing. When she was elected KPD chairwoman, he joined the Zentrale. He was a member of the Neukölln city council, of the Prussian parliament, and also briefly of the Reichstag.

Grylewicz was expelled from the KPD in 1927 alongside the rest of the left opposition. But while Fischer recanted and attempted to reconcile with Stalin, Grylewicz set out to build a new communist organization. He joined the International Left Opposition, led by Leon Trotsky, and in 1930, he was a founding member of the German Trotskyist group: the United Left Opposition of the KPD (Bolshevik-Leninists) (VLO). The Trotskyist weekly paper *Permanente Revolution* was published from Grylewicz's apartment, as well as Trotsky's pamphlets.

As the Nazi party grew, the two main workers' parties refused to close ranks, even for basic self-defense. The social democrats called the communists "red fascists." The communists called the social democrats "social fascists." And it goes without saying that you can't join with fascists to fight other fascists.

Trotsky and Grylewicz were agitating for a workers' united front against fascism, a policy developed by the early Communist International. As Trotsky wrote:

> Communist workers must say to their Social Democratic counterparts: 'The policies of our parties are irreconcilably opposed; but if the fascists come tonight to wreck your organization's hall, we will come running, arms in hand, to help you. Will you promise us that if our organization is threatened you will rush to our aid?' This is the quintessence of our policy in the present period.

In early 1933, Nazi stormtroopers ransacked Grylewicz's apartment. He fled to Czechoslovakia, and in 1937 to France, and in 1941 to Cuba. He and his wife remained on the island until 1955, when they returned to West Berlin. Grylewicz dropped out of politics around 1937, but he survived until 1971, just long enough to see a new Trotskyist movement emerge in West Berlin. Starting in 1968, radical students would visit him to learn from his experiences.

In June 2021, I got two Stolpersteine placed in front of this building for Anton and Anna-Maria Grylewicz.

4.10. *Bloody May Day*
Hermannstraße, corner of Herrfurthstraße

Hermannstraße is Neukölln's busiest street: a constant flow of traffic heading down to the Autobahn, between apartment buildings and a number of cemeteries. To understand why the communists and the social democrats failed to unite against the growing Nazi threat, it helps to look at a massacre that took place here: the Blutmai (Bloody May) of 1929.

Berlin first celebrated International Workers Day on May 1, 1890 — one year after the holiday was proclaimed by the Socialist International. That day, August Bebel spoke to an indoor rally at the Neue Welt in Neukölln. For the next 40 years, Berlin workers staged strikes and protests on this day, with only a brief interruption during World War I. But in 1929, Berlin's social democratic police chief Karl Zörgiebel prohibited all public gatherings. Especially in the red districts like Wedding and Neukölln, this was an unheard-of provocation. Tens of thousands of proletarians defied the ban.

Thousands of police were on the streets with orders to break up any meeting. Confrontations took place all along Hermannstraße and down at the S-Bahn station Neukölln. The police deployed armored cars with machine guns, and an eyewitness saw one on Hermannstraße at the corner of what was then Ziethenstraße firing into the upper floors of the apartment buildings.

In the Rollbergviertel, streetlights and cobblestones were torn out to build barricades. Workers fought the police on the evening of May 1, and on the next evening as well. Over the course of those two days, police shot at least 11,000 rounds of ammunition. Between 32 and 38 civilians were killed. A number of victims had not even been on the streets — they were shot in their homes.

The police claimed that the reds had fired first. The number of injured police? Zero. Eventually one police officer with a bullet wound was presented. But the press soon discovered that he had shot himself with his own gun days before May 1. While the police blamed the Communist Party for organizing a riot, only a tenth of the 1,200 people arrested that day were KPD members.

No one — neither police officers nor politicians — was ever charged with a crime. There was no parliamentary, criminal, or civil investigation. The closest we have gotten to an official reckoning is the first season of the TV show *Babylon Berlin*, which was partially sponsored by German public TV. The beautiful communist demonstration they staged on Hermannplatz is, unfortunately, not historically accurate. There was far too much police violence for thousands of workers to gather with banners and flags like that. But the massacre was displayed exactly as it happened.

4.11. Comenius Garden
Comenius-Garten — Richardstraße 35

This tranquil garden, with willows, a gazebo, and a statue of the Czech theologian John Amos Comenius, might look like it was once part of a monastery from the days of old Rixdorf. It is in fact quite new — from 1995. This used to be the site of Neukölln's biggest tenement, known as the Richardsburg (Richard Castle). Over 500 people lived in 144 apartments surrounding five courtyards.

A bar stood on the ground floor facing out onto the street. In the Weimar Republic, political parties had countless meeting places. These were often private taverns where the owner would strike a deal with a party: They could hang up their flags and posters in exchange for paying part of the rent. The owner of this particular bar, Heinrich Böwe, was facing hard times. Due to the economic crisis of 1929, many of his proletarian customers were unemployed and not paying their debts.

At the same time, the Nazi party under its Berlin leader Joseph Goebbels was trying to gain a foothold in red districts like Wedding and Neukölln. The Nazi stormtroopers of the SA made Böwe an offer: He could turn his bar into a Sturmlokal, and they would purchase a minimum of 30 tons of beer per month.

Böwe agreed, and a nightmare began for the residents of the Richardsburg. At least 30 uniformed, drunken Nazis gathered in their building from morning till night. Fascists urinated in doorways and threatened residents with guns. The neighbors set up a Hausschutzstafel (home defense squad) that united communist, social democratic, and independent workers — an example of a local united front. Every day there were antifascist protests in front of the Nazified bar. Neighbors launched a rent strike demanding the landlord throw Böwe out.

On October 15, 1931, at one such confrontation, Böwe was hit by a stray bullet and died. The police arrested 32 people but were not able to convict anyone for murder. In early 1932, a number of the SA's Sturmlokale were prohibited by the Berlin government, including this one.

When the Nazis came to power a year later, they were out for revenge against Neukölln's working class. The convictions from 1932 were ignored, and the Nazis launched a new "Richardstraße Trial." It began in 1935 and lasted for six months. In the end, five workers were condemned to death: Helmut Schweers, Bruno Blank, Bruno Schröter, Walter Schulz, and Paul Zimmermann. A Stolperstein was recently placed for Schulz at Donaustraße 114.

The Richardsburg tenement was torn down in 1971. After the lot stood empty for many years, it was eventually replaced by the garden.

4.12. Emil Linke
Böhmische Straße 28a

Opposite the Comenius Garden we can enter a small street known as Kirchgasse (church alley). Passing the statue of Friedrich Wilhelm I, we go through an arch into a hidden but public garden. Leaving this garden to the north, we end up on Bohemian Street. This is, according to the Nazi prosecutors from 1935, where the communist hit squad fled after killing Böwe. Not that their version of events is to be believed...

A simple white building in this street was once home to Emil Linke, a worker who was a member of the KPD's sub-district leadership for Neukölln. Five leading Neukölln communists, including Linke, were charged in the Richardstraße Trial — in addition to the five workers who were accused of having fired the shot. The leaders were tried in absentia, as they had fled the country in 1933. In exile in Prague, they held a public counter-trial.

The Nazis reported on their show trial on the front pages of their central organ, the *Völkischer Beobachter*. Their goal was to convict the top KPD leadership of murder in the eyes of the world. Walter Ulbricht, who had been the head of the KPD's Berlin organization (and would go on to lead the German Democratic Republic), was accused of having given the order to shoot Heinrich Böwe. The Nazis intended to place the ultimate blame on the KPD's chairman Ernst Thälmann.

The whole thing was an obvious forgery. While it's certainly plausible that Ulbricht had encouraged the Neukölln communists to take off the gloves when dealing with local Nazis, this does not add up to a murder plot. Had Thälmann been ordering assassinations, would he have really started with an opportunist barkeep in Neukölln?

The five Neukölln communist leaders were convicted of murder, but they were safely outside of Germany. A number of them ended up in the Soviet Union, hoping to build socialism. But Emil Linke was arrested by the Soviet secret service in 1938. Having fought against the Nazis in Neukölln and been driven into exile, he now stood accused of being a German spy! Two years later, he was executed by a Stalinist firing squad. The same thing happened to a number of his comrades who had escaped the Richarstraße Trial: Albert Hein was shot in 1938 and Josef Erdmann in 1941.

This was, after all, the time of the Hitler-Stalin pact. Hundreds of German communists in Soviet exile were handed over to the Gestapo. Many others were executed by Stalin's henchmen. As the historian Hermann Weber has calculated, between 1919 and 1945, a total of 59 communists served on the KPD's top leadership. Of these 59, Hitler killed six, but Stalin killed seven or eight!

4.13. *Karl Marx Square*
Karl-Marx-Platz

There are not too many streets or squares named after Karl Marx in West Germany. But here we have one of each. Karl-Marx-Platz is a tiny, triangular square that hosts a weekly market.

Where does the name come from? Right after World War II, before the Cold War started, the Allies agreed to get rid of old names related to the Kaiser. And why not offer a gift to the workers of this still very red district?

The square had been called Hohenzollernplatz, and it was changed to Karl-Marx-Platz in 1945. Within just a few years, the Western powers abandoned this policy, and that is why West Berlin is still full of names of Prussian kings. But here, Marx has held out.

The street was originally known as Berliner Straße and Bergstraße. It was renamed Karl-Marx-Straße in 1946. There is a relief of Karl Marx's face above the entrance of Karl-Marx-Straße 1, looking down on the Dunkin' Donuts on Hermannplatz.

This tiny square was the site of a historic demonstration. In 1968, a new left was emerging in West Berlin: the Extra-Parliamentary Opposition (APO). On April 11, 1968, one of the main leaders of the Berlin student movement, Rudi Dutschke, was shot by a right-wing terrorist. (See Stop 5.9)

After that assassination attempt, the movement radicalized. For International Workers' Day, they decided to organize their own independent demonstration. This was the first time since the founding of the Federal Republic of Germany that the left would demonstrate separately from the German Trade Union Confederation (DGB). Times were a'changing, but official union leaders strongly supported the U.S. war in Vietnam. The APO wanted to take their anti-imperialist message ("Amis out of Vietnam!") to a workers' district, and called for a demonstration at Karl-Marx-Platz.

No one knew if anyone would show up — such a thing had never been attempted before. On May 1, the tiny square was overflowing with 30,000 people — just as many as at the union demonstration. Old communist workers hung old red flags out of their windows. A gathering like this hadn't taken place since 1932, a whole generation earlier.

Tens of thousands of people at the May Day demonstration of the Extra-Parliamentary Opposition in 1968 at Karl-Marx-Platz in Neukölln. See Stop 4.13. Copyright Jürgen Henschel. Courtesy of the Friedrichshain-Kreuzberg Museum.

4.14. Syndikat
Weisestraße 56

As of this writing, the storefront at Weisestraße 56 is abandoned. Signs for the beer brands Flensburger Pilsner and Jever show that this was once a bar. Graffiti commemorates the fact that this was not just any bar…

Syndikat opened in the mid-1980s. This anarchist bar, run as a collective, was full of smoke, punk music, and a large pool table. This did not used to be a nice neighborhood: For decades, planes landing at Tempelhof airport would fly right above the roofs. But once the airport closed and was turned into a park in 2010, that changed overnight. (See Stop 10.1)

In 2018, after more than 30 years in business, Syndikat was told they were going to be evicted. The building's new owner was a shell company with a letterbox in Luxemburg. It took a lot of research to figure out this was actually the Pears Group, a realty company based in London that controls something like six billion pounds worth of property.

Protests went on for years under the slogan "Syndikat bleibt!" (Syndikat will remain!), which can still be seen spray painted on walls across Berlin. In August 2020, 1,000 Berlin police shut down Weisestraße to carry out the eviction. If you look today, the storefront is likely still abandoned — no one would want to open a gallery at an address that will be remembered by angry leftists for many years.

This shows, in a way, how little has changed in Neukölln. Just like in 1929, we still have a social democratic government — this time with two social democratic parties in power instead of one (the SPD has been joined by DIE LINKE). They talk about reforms and even socialism, but when the interests of big capitalists are at stake, police come out *en masse* to beat up working-class people.

Rosa Luxemburg and Karl Liebknecht are said to have gone into hiding in Neukölln. (See Stop 3.9) On the run from proto-fascist paramilitaries, they spent two nights in the tiny apartment of a working-class family. Later recollections of those days did not include the family's name and address, to protect them from the Nazis. Rumors say they stayed at Weisestraße 8, almost directly opposite the former Syndikat.

Throughout history, lots of important revolutionary meetings have taken place in the back rooms of Neukölln bars. On the morning of November 2, 1918, for example, the Revolutionary Stewards sat down in a bar on Boddinstraße to plan the insurrection that took place one week later. That address, unfortunately, has been lost to history as well.

Now the Syndikat is gone. But there are plenty of other lefty bars to choose from in Neukölln — and many more revolutionary actions to plan.

Rudi Dutschke on February 21, 1968. See Stop 5.1. Photograph by Ben van Meerendonk. CC BY-SA 2.0. Courtesy of IISG, Amsterdam.

1968 in West Berlin

5.1. Amerika-Haus
Hardenbergstraße 22

If you arrived in Berlin after the year 2000, you've probably never had a reason to go to City West and Kurfürstendamm. This neighborhood, full of retirees in bougie cafés and Russian oligarchs shopping for luxury brands, feels like a different and less interesting city. It is hard to imagine that this was once the pulsing center of Western imperialism's most far-flung outpost. It's even harder to picture that all the radical protests from 50 years ago took place here.

The Amerika-Haus, opposite the world-famous train station Bahnhof Zoo, is one place where Berlin's post-war radicalization kicked off. In the 1960s, a quarter of a million U.S. soldiers were stationed in West Germany. That military might was buttressed by lots of soft power. The Amerika-Haus, run by the U.S. government, offered books, magazines, lectures, and exhibitions to sell American culture and democratic values to de-Nazified Germany. My father, an exchange student in West Germany in 1963, came to the Amerika-Haus for a Fourth of July celebration. After a year of eating German sausages, he had forgotten just how bad authentic American hotdogs were, with mystery meat, squishy buns, and bright yellow mustard.

As the Vietnam War heated up in the 1960s, the centrally-located Amerika-Haus was the perfect place for Berliners to register their opposition — protests at the U.S. Embassy down in Dahlem would have been seen by no one. (See Stop 1.13) On February 5, 1966, a few thousand people blocked Hardenbergstraße in front of the Amerika-Haus to protest against the "dirty war in Vietnam." They had started at the Maison de France, a similar institution of French imperialism that still exists at Kurfürstendamm 211. After marching to the Amerika-Haus, they pulled down the Stars and Stripes.

Demonstrators called for negotiations with the National Liberation Front of South Vietnam (more commonly known in English as the Viet Cong) and "peace instead of diplomatic lies." One person started throwing eggs at the building, and this was a huge shock for the residents of the Front-Line City, who were taught to see the U.S. military as their protectors against a Soviet invasion. The western half of the city had always been wealthy and more right-wing.

The driving force behind this first protest was a 26-year-old sociology student at the Free University. Rudi Dutschke was originally from a village near Luckenwalde in East Germany, but moved to the West just three days before the wall went up. He became a member of the situationist group Subversive Action, which then joined the Socialist German Student League (SDS).

To mobilize, Dutschke and fellow activist Bernd Rabehl put up posters all around the city: "[Chancellor Ludwig] Erhard and the parties in Bonn are supporting murder. Murder by napalm bombs. Murder by poison gas. U.S. aggression in Vietnam goes against the interests of the democratic system. Cuba, Congo,

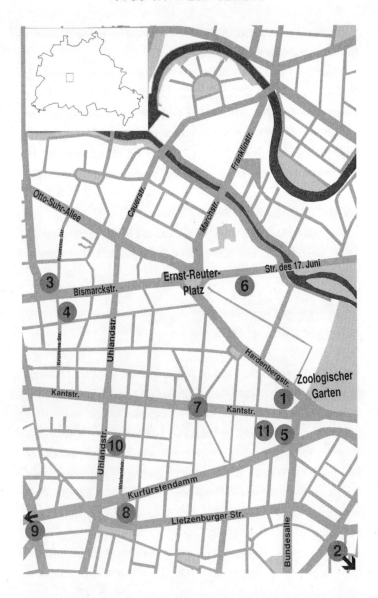

Vietnam — the capitalists' answer is war. *Amis out of Vietnam!* International Liberation Front."

This poster contained all the contours of Germany's emerging student movement, which identified with the liberation movements in the Third World. Trapped between two systems, in a capitalist enclave surrounded by a Stalinist wall, they began talking about the creation of an "association of free individuals, independent of capitalist and Stalinist bureaucrats, in a Free State of West Berlin." This was their counterproposal to Khrushchev's demand that West Berlin become a "free city."

The Amerika-Haus was closed in 2006. In 2014, the photography gallery C/O Berlin moved in, as did Berlin's State Agency for Civic Education.

5.2. *Schöneberg City Hall*
Rathaus Schöneberg — Am Rathaus 2

On May 27, 1967, the Shah of Persia arrived for a state visit in West Berlin. Mohammad Reza Pahlavi and his wife Farah Pahlavi were the Kennedys of the Middle East: He was the scion of a 2,500-year-old dynasty, and she was a fashion icon. The Shah's ex-wife, Soraya, was particularly famous in Europe, as her father had been the Iranian ambassador to Germany and her mother was from Berlin. After the Shah divorced her in 1958, she lived in Germany and France, with frequent appearances in the tabloid press.

There were a number of Iranian students in West Berlin, and they came out to protest alongside German students when the Shah visited the city hall in Schöneberg. This grey building, under a monumental clock tower, was built in 1914 when Schöneberg was still an independent city. After World War II and the division of Berlin, this became the seat of West Berlin's government — Kennedy gave his "Ich bin ein Berliner" speech here in 1963.

On the afternoon of June 2, 1967, around 2,000 people gathered behind police barricades opposite the city hall. Most of them were there to get a glimpse of the famous couple — perhaps 400 intended to protest. So there was a mix of signs: both "Welcome to Berlin" and "Welcome to Berlin, Mister Dictator!"

The Iranian secret service, the SAVAK, had flown 80 agents into West Berlin. They arrived in Schöneberg in buses and stood around in dark suits holding pro-Shah signs in Farsi and German — except the German lettering was childish, written by people unfamiliar with the Latin alphabet. The press called them "Jubelperser" (cheering Persians).

All of a sudden, these Iranian agents took the sticks from their signs and began to beat demonstrators. They actually ended up beating fans of the Shah as well, since they couldn't tell the difference. The police let them rampage for several minutes. They were thus rechristened "Prügelperser" (beating Persians). This was a bit of a scandal: Why had the German government let a foreign secret service beat German citizens on German territory? But the day was just beginning!

5.3. German Opera
Deutsche Oper — Bismarckstraße 35

The bleak, towering facade on Bismarckstraße states its purpose in simple black letters: German Opera. The outside looks like a nuclear bunker, but the inside houses an elegant, wood-paneled theater. The building was opened in 1961, as Berlin's two main operas had ended up in the East — that is why the city now has three.

A few hours after their trip to Schöneberg on June 2, the Shah and the Shahbanu attended a performance of Mozart's *The Magic Flute*. Accompanied by Germany's federal president, they arrived at the opera by limousine a few minutes before 8 p.m.

Directly across the street from the opera, on a sidewalk which is now in front of a massive concrete apartment tower, a few hundred demonstrators had assembled. They carried signs like: "Murderers out of West Berlin!" and "Down with the Shah!" They chanted slogans and threw a couple of eggs when the cars pulled up. But the monarchs were whisked into the opera without incident.

Police barricades stood in front of the demonstrators, while a construction fence was behind them, leaving just a narrow strip for free speech. Now that the opera had begun, what were the demonstrators going to do? Would they stand around for more than three hours for the Shah to emerge again? So that they could chant slogans for another three minutes? If they were anything like me, they were already debating about which bar to go to.

At 8:04 p.m., without warning, police jumped over the barricades and began beating protesters with batons. Trapped between the barricades and the fence, there was nowhere for them to flee. West Berlin's police chief Erich Duensing had planned this exactly. He had come up with the idea while eating breakfast: If you push a knife into the middle of a Leberwurst, he noticed, its contents will spill out both sides — hence the "Leberwurst tactic" of striking the demonstration at the center.

Duensing, by the way, was a recipient of the Nazis' highest military honor, the Knight's Cross of the Iron Cross. He had served on the general staff of the Army Group South, which was responsible for scorched earth and mass murder in Ukraine. Many of his police commanders were former SS and Wehrmacht officers. Before June 2, he had declared that "the time of patience with communists is over."

As cops were kicking people and dragging them across the ground, a police loudspeaker announced that an officer had been stabbed. That was a lie — to this day, it's not clear if such a lie had been part of the plan.

That evening, West Berlin's mayor Heinrich Albertz put out a press release: "The police, provoked by hooligans, were forced to ... use their batons. I explicitly and emphatically state that I approve of the behavior of the police." He was approving of more than just beatings.

The demonstrators slowly managed to escape from either side of the kettle. Many of them ran south into Krumme Straße (literally: Crooked Street). The 27-year-old student Benno Ohnesorg was at his very first demonstration, along with his pregnant wife, carrying a banner that said, "For the autonomy for the University of Tehran." We can now follow the path they took, 150 meters to the south, imagining that we are full of rage and passion as we flee from rampaging cops.

5.4. Benno Ohnesorg
Krumme Straße 66

The post-war apartment building at Krumme Straße 66 is raised on concrete pillars above a parking lot — an architectural style that did not catch on in West Berlin. Today, cars parked under the building are blocked off by a fence. In the 1960s, the lot was open.

Pausing in front of this building, Christa Ohnesorg said she needed to go home. Benno replied that he wanted to observe plainclothes police arresting a demonstrator. He went under the building and stood against a wall. When he tried to leave, he was surrounded by three police officers who began to beat him.

Suddenly, a shot rang out. An man in a suit was standing 1.5 meters behind Ohnesorg with his arm extended. He had shot the young man in the back of the head. This was Karl-Heinz Kurras of the political police. It's not entirely clear why he pulled the trigger. One witness thought they heard him say the gun had gone off by itself. In court, he claimed that it was — what else? — "self-defense." Like almost all police murderers, Kurras was cleared of any wrongdoing.

There is a famous picture of a young woman in an elegant black dress and large earrings kneeling over Ohnesorg's body. His banner is rolled up under his head and covered in blood. She later recalled that a number of protesters had come in evening wear, in an unsuccessful attempt to get into the opera and stage a protest inside. Ohnesorg died in the ambulance on the way to the hospital. One week later, on June 9, 10,000 people attended his funeral in Hannover. Soon, West Berlin's police chief, mayor, and interior senator all had to resign.

In 2009, it was revealed that Kurras had been a long-time agent of the East German secret service inside the West Berlin police. Had the Stasi planned this murder, in order to radicalize the student movement? We can say with certainty: no. The Stasi had zero interest in Ohnesorg's death — they lost a very important source in the Western security apparatus. When he committed the murder, Kurras was acting as a West German police officer, not as an East German spy. And when the courts absolved him of all charges, he was being protected as a West Berlin police officer.

June 2 marked a before and an after in the history of the Federal Republic. That shot radicalized an entire generation in West Germany. The only thing we can compare it to is when a younger generation was forced to watch the police murder George Floyd in 2020. Today, a plaque at Krumme Straße 66 recounts the murder of Ohnesorg — a large statue in front of the opera is also dedicated to him.

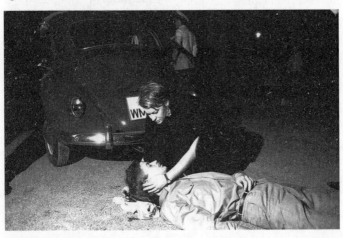

Benno Ohnesorg dying at Krumme Straße 66 on June 2, 1967. See Stop 5.4. Photographer unknown. Via Wikimedia Commons.

5.5. Kranzler Eck
Kurfürstendamm 18

For young people in Berlin today, Ku'damm is basically invisible (unless you are one of those deeply alienated young men who enjoy drag racing through the City West). Fifty years ago, half the city would come here every Saturday to stroll. Café Kranzler Eck, with its rotunda and candy-striped awnings, was the place where elderly war widows would meet for coffee and cake. The history of the coffee house goes all the way back to 1834 — this eye-catching location was opened in 1958. Today the building is mostly occupied by retail chains offering assorted tchotchkes.

Starting in 1967, students would gather on this corner on Saturday afternoons. They would break out into agitation groups of 10 or 15 to hand out fliers about Vietnam, democracy, or other controversial topics. According to one veteran, about 90% of passersby were actively hostile. A common response was: "You should all be gassed!" More restrained Berliners would tell them to "go over to the other side" (of the wall). Just 5% of people were neutral, while 5% expressed sympathy. West Berlin, after all, was a very conservative city — even the radical students would usually be wearing a coat and tie, or a long dress.

These actions were organized by the AStA, the student governments of the Free University and the Technical University. Or by the SDS, which had once been the student organization of the Social Democratic Party (SPD) but was expelled in 1961. This aligned very closely with the United States, where the main organization of the student movement was also called SDS — there it was Students for a Democratic Society. Both SDSes started out as fairly small student groups connected to reformist bureaucracies. They grew explosively in 1968, becoming big tents for the entire radical movement, and then quickly splintered into a thousand pieces. Rudi Dutschke from the German SDS was married to Gretchen Klotz, an American from the other SDS.

The students were part of the Extra-Parliamentary Opposition (APO). A "grand coalition" had come to power in Bonn in 1966, uniting the SPD and the conservative CDU. The government thus controlled 95% of seats in the Bundestag — and the only opposition would have to come from outside parliament. Students started protesting about all kinds of things: the authoritarian structures at the universities, the continuities with the Nazi regime, and the war in Vietnam.

Young people would disrupt Christmas shopping on Ku'damm or burst into Café Kranzler Eck where they would snatch pieces of cake from diners. The idea was to shock people and help them abandon bourgeois modes of thinking.

October 21, 1967 was an international day of action against the war in Vietnam. On that day, 100,000 people demonstrated outside the Pentagon in Washington, D.C. In West Berlin, just 7,000 came out — but that was a lot for this city. Dutschke gave a speech, as did French, Greek, Arab, and American activists. Che Guevara had been killed two weeks earlier, and his picture was everywhere. His slogan had been: "Create Two, Three, Many Vietnams!" That is what the German students were trying to do — and, at the very least, they blocked Ku'damm.

5.6. Technical University
Technische Universität — Straße des 17. Juni 135

The sprawling campus of the Technical University (TU) opened in 1879 as the Royal Technical Academy of Berlin. The main building is a labyrinth — the oldest parts were built in 1888, while others were completed a century later. The atrium in the middle has kept its imperial look, while the main foyer is full of exposed concrete, as was the style in the 1960s. If we stand facing the glass facade of the main building, an enormous block covered in metal cladding juts out on the lower left. This is the Audimax — short for auditorium maximum, which is Latin for "biggest lecture hall." From the inside, the Audimax is an austere, brutalist space — but over the years it has been full of revolutionary energy.

The political center of the West Berlin student movement was the Free University — but that was all the way down in Dahlem, half an hour away by subway. If a few thousand Berlin radicals needed to meet up, there was no better place than TU. The student government, the AStA, would provide space and printing facilities. Every year on July 4, the U.S. Army would hold a parade down Straße des 17. Juni. The AStA would hang speakers out their windows in the main building and blast the Internationale and other revolutionary songs — by 1973, the military was forced to abandon their ritual.

In 1967, students started holding "teach-ins" here every Wednesday, copying the format from U.S. colleges. On February 1, 1968, a "Springer Tribunal" was on the agenda — a public hearing about the nefarious influence of Axel Springer. He was the Rupert Murdoch of West Germany: His sensationalist, misogynistic, right-wing tabloids controlled 70% of the newspaper market in West Berlin.

This was planned as a sociological discussion. But before the event started, a five-minute black-and-white film was projected on stage: "How do I build a molotov cocktail?" This instructional video was made by a film student named Holger Meins — who would soon become a founding member of the Red Army Faction (RAF). This showed the two directions the student movement was pulling: debating the ideological influence of media monopolies — or smashing the windows of those same monopolies. Rudi Dutschke was a unifying figure because he could discuss the ideas of Lukács and Gramsci, but also drag a mounted police officer down off his horse.

Two weeks later, on February 17–18, TU was the site of the International Vietnam Congress. Up to 6,000 people attended — half came from West Berlin and the other half from West Germany or further abroad. This was just a few weeks after the Tet Offensive had shown people around the world that the U.S. military could be defeated.

In the packed Audimax, speakers included: Alain Krivine from Paris of the Revolutionary Communist Youth (JCR), who just three months later would be one of the public faces of the "night of the barricades"; Tariq Ali from London, a Pakistani student who one month later would lead a demonstration of 100,000 against the war; Bernardine Dohrn from Chicago, a member of the American SDS who would soon found the Weather Underground Organization; Peter Weiss, the German author living in Swedish exile; and Ernest Mandel from Brussels, an economist and leader of the Fourth International. Mandel gave enormously popular lectures on "late capitalism" at Berlin's Free University. In 1972, however, Mandel was banned from entering West Germany. He still managed to get his PhD from the FU after his professors travelled to Belgium for the defense.

A speaker from the Student Non-Violent Coordinating Committee in the U.S. said people needed to go "from protest to resistance." This slogan was taken up by the journalist Ulrike Meinhof, who was at the event as a radical reporter and soon founded the RAF. The congress resolved to create a "second revolutionary front against imperialism in its metropolis." An enormous banner in red and light blue, the colors of the National Liberation Front, covered the stage. It had a quote from Che Guevara: "The duty of every revolutionary is to make the revolution."

The students wanted to reach out to U.S. soldiers in Germany, as resistance by G.I.s was growing everywhere — by 1970, there was even an underground G.I. newspaper in Berlin called *Up against the wall*. On February 18, the second day of the congress, they planned to march to the U.S. barracks in Dahlem. The commanders announced they were prepared to shoot live ammunition at anyone approaching their headquarters.

A deadly showdown seemed inevitable. There were backroom negotiations between a part of the police leadership and a part of the SDS leadership, mediated by a bishop and a theology professor. They agreed that if the demonstration were moved to Ku'damm, then the Senate would lift the general ban on protests. So on February 18, 15,000 people marched down Ku'damm chanting "Ho, ho, ho chi minh!" The *Berliner Morgenpost*, a

Springer paper, reported: "Berlin must not be allowed to become Saigon!"

Four days later, the Senate of West Berlin called for a counter-demonstration against the students, with the support of the SPD, the CDU, and the union bureaucracies. Public sector workers got the day off, and 80,000 people came to the city hall in Schöneberg. A sign referred to Rudi Dutschke as "Enemy of the People #1" — a disturbing slogan in a country run by former Nazis. Soon, the crowd began attacking young men with long hair thinking they were Dutschke. The funny thing is Rudi Dutschke's hair wasn't even particularly long, at least not by today's standards. At this government demonstration against "rioters" and "extremists," over 30 people were injured. Different intellectuals later accused the Berlin government of creating an "atmosphere of pogrom."

The International Vietnam Congress at the Technical University on February 17, 1968. The speaker appears to be Tariq Ali. See Stop 5.6. Photograph by Ludwig Binder. CC BY-SA 2.0. Courtesy of Haus der Geschichte.

5.7. Booksellers' Square
Savignyplatz

This small square, bisected by Kantstraße, is a hangout for pensioners and the occasional tourist. Fifty years ago, this was a center of Berlin radicalism. After every teach-in at the Technical University, students would stream down to Savignyplatz. The plaza was filled with bars, left-wing bookshops, and offices of political groups. Only a few of these locations are still around.

The bars Dicke Wirtin (Fat Hostess) and Zwiebelfisch (Onion Fish) are still going strong. Long ago, these were run-down establishments full of smoke and shouting, where a poor student who wanted to argue about Horkheimer or Brezhnev could get a beer or a slice of bread for 50 pfennig. Another restaurant that is still around is Terzo Mondo. It was opened by Kostas, a Greek communist who had fought with the partisans before moving to Berlin.

Post-war Charlottenburg was full of once-luxurious buildings. These were no longer up to modern standards, with toilets in the stairwells and coal stoves. Plus, large swaths of the bourgeoisie had abandoned West Berlin. Students could therefore rent enormous apartments cheaply. They just needed to assemble some bookshelves out of cinderblocks and hang up a few posters — and a communal living space was born.

Charlottenburg was not where workers lived. West Berlin's downtrodden were in districts like Kreuzberg, Wedding, and Neukölln. Some of the most dedicated student activists moved to those neighborhoods in the early 1970s to be among the working class. We tend to think of Kreuzberg as the radical part of West Berlin, but Kreuzberg didn't get that reputation until the 1980s — in the 1960s, Kreuzberg was a place for immigrant workers. Christian Ströbele, who came to be Kreuzberg's most famous resident as the local Green Party MP (See Stop 6.8), has said he never went to Kreuzberg during the years of the student movement.

5.8. Republican Club
Wielandstraße 27

We are now at the absolute worst part of Ku'damm, surrounded by Louis Vuitton and Prada. At Wielandstraße 27, on the first floor, was the office of the Republican Club. This was the central organizing space of the 1968 movement: a repurposed 12-room apartment.

The Republican Club had been founded by liberal and leftist intellectuals who were sympathetic to the APO, but a bit older than the students. Their club provided infrastructure to the entire movement. Fifteen-year-olds who wanted to publish an anti-authoritarian newspaper at their school could come here to print it by hand. The club also did a campaign in support of conscientious objectors to military service. They were successful, and as a result, young men in West Berlin did not have to serve in the Bundeswehr, the West German army.

This apartment also served as the meeting place of the Action Committee for Women's Liberation, launched at the beginning of 1968. This was the first organization of the second-wave feminist movement in Berlin. Their founding statement declared:

147

"We must stop trying to solve the misery individually, or waiting for the time after the revolution."

The young feminists protested against the student movement's ignorance of women's oppression, declaring that "the private is political." In September 1968, the SDS held its national conference in Frankfurt am Main. A member of the Action Committee, Helke Sander, demanded in a speech that the organization take up "the specific problems of women." The next speaker, SDS chief theoretician Hans-Jürgen Krahl, didn't take up the topic at all. Sigrid Rüger had a famous response: She threw a tomato, shouting, "Comrade Krahl, you are a reactionary!" She later explained that she "threw the tomato to encourage girls to emotionally and aggressively articulate their problems." This fruit marked the beginning of Germany's new women's movement.

The Action Committee for Women's Liberation set up Kinderläden (literally: children's shops) in different parts of Berlin. With corner grocers being replaced by supermarkets, countless storefronts were empty. These were taken over to offer self-organized childcare. By 1969, there were 15 of them around the city. This wasn't just about giving women more freedom — the idea was also to provide emancipatory education for children.

5.9. SDS Headquarters
Kurfürstendamm 142

1.5 kilometers further down Ku'damm, we would have reached the SDS headquarters, where the leadership also lived communally. Like the Republican Club, this was nothing more than an old apartment. The building is no longer there — it was replaced by public housing. A metal plaque in the sidewalk, in front of the Waage Apotheke (pharmacy), commemorates what happened here.

On April 11, 1968, a 23-year-old from Munich named Josef Bachmann went to the SDS office. He waited outside, and before long Rudi Dutschke pulled up on his bicycle. Dutschke was not supposed to be in the office that day — he had come up from his apartment in Dahlem to get nose drops for his son Hosea Che from the pharmacy next door.

Bachman asked: "Are you Rudi Dutschke?" Dutschke said that he was. Bachmann pulled a gun and shot him three times, including one shot to the head. He was taken to a hospital and, after a five-hour operation, barely survived. Over the next few months, Dutschke slowly learned to speak and to walk again while in exile in an Italian villa. Unable to stand the hate-filled atmosphere in West Berlin, he and his family moved to England, but he was expelled in 1971 as an "undesirable alien." He then moved to Aarhus in Denmark. In 1979, he had a seizure in the bathtub and drowned.

The shooting happened less than a week after Martin Luther King Jr. had been assassinated in Memphis. Riots were taking place all over the United States. With images of militant resistance in their heads, 2,500 people filled the Audimax at TU that evening. An isolated right-winger had pulled the trigger — but who had instigated Bachmann to commit murder? The guy, after all, was not even from Berlin. Bachman had been carrying an issue of the right-wing newspaper *National-Zeitung* with the headline: "Stop Dutschke now! Otherwise there will be civil war." Springer's *Bild* had written: "We can't leave the dirty work to the police and their water cannons." From a moral perspective, Springer was responsible for the attempted murder.

This was a Thursday — the Thursday before the four-day Easter weekend. The students marched to the Springer building in Kreuzberg and began flipping over delivery trucks. While they smashed windows, an agent of the West German secret service was handing out molotov cocktails (more on that in a second). These protests became known as the Easter Riots. Up to 60,000 people participated in blockades to stop the *Bild* newspaper from being delivered. The demand was to "expropriate Springer." This was, by an astounding coincidence, almost exactly 50 years after Spartacists had briefly occupied a right-wing tabloid at the same location. (See Stop 3.8)

5.10. *Wieland Commune*
Wielandstraße 13

This elegant white building, covered in classical statues, is not where you would expect to find a bunch of revolutionary dope fiends. A massive apartment on the first floor on the right was nonetheless home to one of the numerous communes being founded by radical students. The most famous of these, the Kommune 1, was based at different addresses, but mostly further to the West (such as at Kaiser-Friedrich-Straße 54A at Stuttgarter Platz). At the same time, Maoist sects were springing up like mushrooms after a rain, and each had a name more pretentious than the last, with combinations of "Communist Party," "Marxist-Leninist," "Central Bureau," etc. The hedonist faction that settled at Wielandstraße 13 found these names amusing and called themselves the Central Council of the Wandering Hashish Rebels.

The Wieland Commune started out as a reading group at the Free University studying Marx's *Capital*. Soon it became a center of counterculture with a particular emphasis on narcotics. Their motto: "Hash, Opium, Heroin — for a free West Berlin!"

Their political discussions fueled by mind-altering substances, in 1969 they decided to carry out propaganda of the deed. They founded an urban guerrilla group, the Tupamaros West Berlin, taking their name from an armed organization in Uruguay. Their first action was at the Jewish Community Center (See Next Stop). It was such a disaster, rejected by the entire Left, that the Tupamaros only attempted one further bombing. They met with the founders of the Red Army Faction, but got stuck with the old left-wing debate about centralism versus autonomy. As a result, there was no fusion. In 1970, the Tupamaros' main leader was arrested, and the group dissolved.

By 1972, a number of former members of the Wieland Commune participated in the formation of the June 2 Movement. The name of this armed group referred to the day in 1967 when Benno Ohnesorg was murdered. They are best remembered for one spectacular action: kidnapping Peter Lorenz, the CDU's candidate for mayor in 1975. Three days before the elections, Lorenz's car was surrounded near his home in Zehlendorf (a plaque at Quermatenweg 128 marks the spot). He was taken to a hiding place at Schenkendorfstraße 7 in Kreuzberg, around the corner from the Marheineke-Halle. The terrorists had actually opened a secondhand shop and sold used clothing for months to provide cover! After five days in this "People's Prison," the German government released five imprisoned RAF members and let them fly to South Yemen. Lorenz was released — and he still lost the elections.

The apartment on Wielandstraße had been rented by Otto Schily, a lawyer who defended student protesters and RAF members. Three decades later, in 1998, Schily became Germany's interior minister. After having defended terrorists, he was responsible for Germany's "anti-terrorism laws" passed after September 11.

One of the members of this commune, Georg von Rauch, was killed by police in 1971. An occupied house was named after him. (See Stop 6.2) Another activist of the June 2 Movement, Tommy Weisbecker, was shot the following year. There is a Tommy-Weisbecker-Haus at Wilhelmstraße 9, opposite the current SPD headquarters.

5.11. Jewish Community Center
Jüdisches Gemeindehaus — Fasanenstraße 80

The Jewish Community Center was opened in 1959 on the site of a synagogue that had been destroyed by the Nazis. November 9, 1969 was the 31st anniversary of the November pogroms (which the Nazis called the Reichskristallnacht — the Night of Broken Glass). A ceremony attracted 250 people. They did not know that a bomb had been placed in the center. The explosive did not detonate — the next day, a cleaner discovered it in the cloak room and called the police.

The previous night, graffiti had appeared in different parts of the city: "Shalom and Napalm." A flier published in the radical left magazine *Agit 883* explained that "racist and Zionist Israel, with napalm ... and German tanks is defending the oil interests of the world police in the entire Arab region." The authors supported Al Fatah, the Palestinian nationalist group led by Yassir Arafat, who were "showing everyone how to fight imperialism, Zionism, and the system in their own countries."

This was the first action of the Tupamaros West Berlin. Dieter Kunzelmann, Georg von Rauch, Tommy Weisbecker and others had gone to Jordan in mid-1969 for guerrilla training at a Palestinian refugee camp. They decided to begin the armed struggle right away. Their first action — less than 25 years after the liberation of Auschwitz — would be to bomb a Jewish community center.

In the late 1960s, European left-wing public opinion about Israel shifted by 180 degrees. When the state of Israel was founded, many saw it as a kind of national liberation project — the Soviet Union under Stalin recognized the new state immediately. It looked like a socialist country with collective farms. That changed overnight with the Six-Day War in 1967. After Israel defeated the nationalist regimes of multiple Arab countries, it was now suddenly perceived as a gendarme of imperialism. Before 1967, progressive European students had visited Israeli *kibbutzim* — now they were going to Palestinian refugee camps. Many in Europe saw Israeli Jews like the French colonists in Algeria, who had been forced to leave in 1961.

This attempted mass murder of Jews in the name of fighting Zionism was quickly condemned by the Republican Club, the

Frankfurt Palestine Committee, and virtually the entire German Left. Except for this one idiotic group, the '68 movement was able to distinguish between Jews and Zionism. Jewish students played a big role in the Europe-wide revolt. The most famous was certainly Daniel Cohn-Bendit. "Dany le Rouge" had been born in France, went to school in Frankfurt, and then to university in Nanterre outside of Paris. He was one of the main faces of the French May, and politicians denounced him as a foreign agitator. In response, demonstrators in Paris chanted: "Nous sommes tous des juifs allemands!" ("We are all German Jews!")

How had the Tupamaros built the bomb? They had help — without realizing it. The explosive had been supplied by Peter Urbach, who had been offering molotov cocktails, pistols, and dynamite to West Berlin's radical scene for years, including in front of the Springer building during the Easter Riots. He was an agent of West Germany's domestic secret service, the cynically named "protectors of the constitution," which had been built up by former Nazis.

The police quickly figured out who was responsible for the attempted bombing, but no one was ever charged. It would have been too much of a scandal for the Federal Republic to admit that its agents had built a bomb that could have killed hundreds of Jews. After he testified in court in 1971, Urbach was unmasked as a spy. The West German government provided him with a new identity, and he moved to California, where he lived off a state pension until his death in 2011.

While conservatives like to claim that West Berlin's '68 movement led to political violence, antisemitism, and child abuse, the truth is that many leading figures went into the bourgeois mainstream. Via a "long march through the institutions" (a phrase coined by Dutschke), former radicals joined the state apparatus. By the late 1990s, prominent '68ers of different stripes were running capitalist Germany. These politicians are now in retirement, writing memoirs denouncing the false idealism of their youth. But celebrities like Joschka Fischer (who became Germany's foreign minister and warmonger-in-chief) should not taint their entire generation. Thousands of rank-and-file activists from 1968 became teachers and social workers. Even if they failed to carry out a revolution, they at least dragged Germany's education system away from late medieval authoritarianism.

The beginning of the Neighborhood Uprising in Kreuzberg on May 1, 1987. See Stop 6.5. Photograph copyright Peter Homann/Umbruch Bildarchiv.

Riots in Kreuzberg

6.1. New Kreuzberg Center
Neues Kreuzberger Zentrum — Kottbusser Tor

Today, Kotti is known for two nefarious ways of making money: gentrification and drugs. A white and yellow colossus wraps around the north side of the square, even stretching across the street, in what looks like a textbook example of failed urban planning. Other buildings are from the late nineteenth century. The population is as eclectic as the architecture: Working-class immigrants — some whose families have been here for generations, and others who just arrived — cross paths with yuppies in their brand-new condos.

We are in the middle of Kreuzberg 36 — named after the old zip code from before German reunification, SO 36. Today, this kiez is right in the middle of Berlin. Between 1961 and 1989, however, it was a last peninsula of the self-proclaimed "free world," practically surrounded by a wall. North of Kotti is the district of Mitte, which was blocked off by a wall. To the east is the Spree, where a wall stood on the opposite bank. To the south-east is a canal that marks the border with Treptow, and there was a wall here as well. Neukölln to the south was wall-free, as this was also part of West Berlin, but there are only four bridges leading over the canal. Thus, the only reliable way in or out of this kiez was to the west: to the other, nicer part of Kreuzberg, known as SW 61.

X-Berg (the "x" stands for the cross in the name — get it?) was not a great neighborhood. The people who ended up living right next to the wall were those who could not afford to live anywhere else, primarily immigrants and students. Starting in the 1960s, millions of so-called Gastarbeiter (guest workers) came to West Germany, first from Italy, then from Greece, and then especially from Turkey. At the same time, the Federal Republic of Germany forced young men into military service. Getting conscientious objector status was difficult — the easiest way to escape the draft was to move to West Berlin, which was officially demilitarized. As a result, West Berlin filled with working-class immigrants and antimilitarist young people, and many of them settled around Kotti.

In the 1950s and 1960s, the kiez consisted largely of run-down buildings from before the war. Starting in the 1970s, these were to be torn down and replaced with modern housing blocks. These buildings would have far higher quality of life — with central heating, elevators, and bathrooms inside the apartments — but also far higher rents. The Neues Kreuzberger Zentrum (NKZ, New Kreuzberg Center), opened in 1974, is a prime example.

With speculators named Schmidt, Press, and Mosch driving up prices in Kreuzberg, rents in these new buildings were four times higher than the local average. It was the plans to replace old housing that launched Kreuzberg's "house struggles." Starting in the 1970s, many residents — not just radical leftists, but also families and owners of small shops — occupied their buildings in

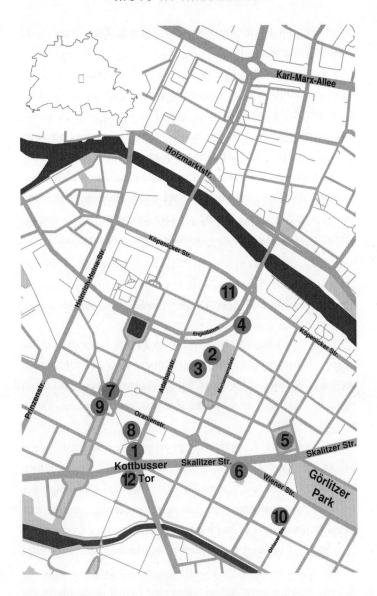

order to prevent them from being torn down. These were called "maintenance occupations."

A massive wave of occupations started in 1980. Soon, there were an estimated 170 occupied buildings in West Berlin with 5,000 people living in them — half of all squats were in Kreuzberg. Today, many of those squats have been evicted — but many were also legalized. Some former squatters are still quite radical, while others have turned into neoliberal Green Party politicians. Lots of old buildings in Kreuzberg were saved by people violating sacred property rights, giving the kiez its mix of late nineteenth century historicism and mid-twentieth century brutalism.

6.2. Georg von Rauch
Georg-von-Rauch-Haus — Mariannenplatz 1A

This massive complex, with red brick turrets lording over the grass of Mariannenplatz, was opened in the 1850s. The Bethanien served as a hospital for more than a century before closing in 1970. In a kiez full of squatters, this was an apple in more than one eye.

On December 8, 1971, young people occupied a building behind the former hospital which had once been a dormitory for nurses. They had gathered at the Technical University for a teach-in about the murder of Georg von Rauch, a member of an urban guerrilla who had been shot by police four days earlier. (See Stop 5.10) They proceeded to Mariannenplatz and christened their new home the Georg-von-Rauch-Haus. Because of this name, right-wing tabloids attempted to link the house to the armed underground, claiming it contained a "bomb workshop." Four months later, the building was stormed by 400 police.

After tearing the place apart for hours, police confirmed at a press conference that they had indeed found evidence of bomb-making: ten empty wine bottles and a canister of gasoline! Ton Steine Scherben, a West Berlin rock band who had participated in the teach-in at TU, were soon performing a historically accurate ballad about the occupation. In the "Rauch-Haus-Song," they explained what police had been thinking: "Ten empty bottles can quickly become ten mollies [molotov cocktails]." That song, recounting the occupation of the Bethanien through the eyes of a working-class everyman named Mensch Meier, ends with the chorus: "And we say it loudly: You won't get us out! This is our house. Throw Schmidt, Press, and Mosch out of Kreuzberg!"

The Rauch-Haus has had contracts with the city since 1971. The building provides housing for young people living on the streets, and also space for parties and concerts. During one such event in 2011, a fire was started, and many suspected arson by Nazis. The damage has since been repaired. As a large graffito on the front of the house points out, this is people's home and not a place for tourists to take selfies.

While that back building was occupied in 1971, the rest of the Bethanien remained empty. The local government realized the only reliable way to prevent further occupations was to fill the space with other people. So in 1973, the main part and the north wing of the former hospital were turned into an Artists' House with studios and galleries. The south wing was used by the Kreuzberg Social Office until 2004. That led to yet another occupation, which we can admire right around the corner.

6.3. *New Yorck*

Marielle-Franco-Platz — Mariannenplatz 2A

Facing the Bethanien and turning to the left, we can go around the corner to the south wing. It's the same building, but this wing has its own radical history that begins on the other side of Kreuzberg. A former factory in the courtyard of Yorckstraße 59 was rented legally in 1988, for what Berliners call a "house project." Such brick buildings in Kreuzberg were once almost worthless, but by the early 2000s, loft apartments were all the rage. A new owner, sensing opportunities for huge profits, decided to throw out the 60 or so people living there.

The inhabitants of the Yorck59 fought courageously to save their home. They occupied the headquarters of the SPD and the PDS, the two governing parties in Berlin, as well as the Victory Column. But after a year of intense protests and fruitless negotiations, one morning in June 2005, 500 police came to evict the building. They broke up a sit-in with such violence that one person was knocked unconscious and taken away in an ambulance.

Five days later, the former residents of the Yorck59 occupied the south wing of the Bethanien. Hence the creative name spray painted on the wall: New Yorck (or: Yorck59 im Exil). This part of the building had been empty since Kreuzberg's Social Office had moved out. The district had been planning to sell the entire complex to private investors.

Immediately after the occupation, something astounding happened: The Berlin police did nothing. Usually they attempt to end any occupation within one hour. Often, they do not even know who owns the property — they just need a reasonable suspicion that it doesn't belong to the people inside. In this case, however, the occupation was tolerated. There are many different theories about why this happened. Were the police hesitant to carry out another brutal eviction while an open-air festival was taking place on Marianenplatz? (That never stopped them before!) Or were the cops deliberately trying to create problems for the "left-wing" district government of Friedrichshain-Kreuzberg? Or did some faceless bureaucrat lack the courage to order an eviction that might cause further serious injuries?

Whatever caused this delay — we will only know for sure after the state's archives are opened after the revolution — it gave the squatters a chance to link up with their neighbors. Before long, a local initiative was organizing a referendum against the plans to privatize the Bethanien. The people from the Artists' House were incensed that the occupiers were not thrown out immediately. In protest, they stopped paying their rent to the district — which is kind of a silly way to protest against squatters, when you think about it. They eventually moved into a new building on Kottbusser Damm, leaving the main part of the Bethanien open to other artists.

The New Yorck is still there, and it was legalized in 2009 — the most successful occupation in Berlin in this millennium. If you go there today, you will likely see political banners hanging out of all the windows. Part of one floor is available for political meetings of all kinds. Another floor provides housing for 60 people — just like the Old Yorck. The small square at the entrance has been renamed for Marielle Franco, a left-wing Black politician in Rio de Janeiro who was assassinated by police in 2018.

6.4. Treehouse at the Wall
Baumhaus an der Mauer — Bethaniendamm

On the north side of Mariannenplatz, just behind the red brick church, we run into a triangular lot with a tree house. Except it's not really a tree house — more of an improvised plywood shed surrounding a tree. This is a remnant from what Kreuzberg used to be. Just behind the hut is the curving street Bethaniendamm/ Engeldamm with a sunken park in the middle. As with just about every long, narrow park in Berlin, this is a place where the wall once stood. (Before that, it was a canal, and the Engelbecken pool remains from those days.)

People assume the wall marked the border between East and West. But as any homeowner would know, the German Democratic Republic (GDR) had to build its wall on its own territory. This meant there was always a small strip of land between the wall and the border. Not only that: The border zigzagged through the city, whereas an effective wall needs to be as straight as possible. That left a few larger pockets of land that belonged to the East but remained on the Western side.

East Berlin police could not readily go over the wall to enforce their laws — yet West Berlin police could not enter foreign territory. These strips and pockets were effectively a legal no-man's land: West Berliners could park cars, take drugs, or make weird art here. No one could do anything about it — except in the rare instance that someone sprayed anti-GDR graffiti, and "People's Police" might leap out of a hidden door in the wall to detain them.

This triangle between the St. Thomas Church at Mariannenplatz and the wall was one such stateless territory. In 1983, a

Turkish immigrant named Osman Kalin cleared out the trash and started planting vegetables. East German border guards paid a visit, and as they were unsure what to do, the question is said to have gotten passed up all the way to the Central Committee of the Socialist Unity Party (SED). They eventually decided that "guerrilla gardening" was no threat to socialism, as long as the hut remained below the height of the wall. Since reunification, the land belongs to the Federal Republic of Germany (FRG). But the church and the district allowed the garden to stay. After Kalin's death in 2018, the Tree House at the Wall passed on to his son.

A larger pocket of statelessness was the Lenné Triangle just south of the Tiergarten and next to Potsdamer Platz (between Lennestraße, Ebertstraße, and Bellevuestraße, which today contains ugly new buildings and the Henriette-Herz-Park). In May 1988, punks and leftists occupied the space. The 200–300 inhabitants could do just about whatever they wanted — anarchy! — as West Berlin police were held back by an invisible line. Cops did, however, surround the field with a fence and repeatedly shoot tear gas inside. The occupiers named their new home the Norbert-Kuback-Triangle — Kuback had been arrested during the Neighborhood Uprising one year earlier (See Stop 6.5), and he was put in solitary confinement for 27 days, driving him to suicide. But the GDR had already agreed to sell this territory to the West. So on July 1, the invisible line disappeared, and the police advanced on "Kubatstan." East German border guards, concerned about the imminent violence by capitalist pigs, lowered ladders over the wall. Many of the occupiers escaped — not many people fled over the wall towards the East! The GDR served them lunch before putting them on the S-Bahn to return to the West individually.

6.5. *Neighborhood Uprising*
Lausitzer Platz

This leafy square around a protestant church, bordered by an elevated U-Bahn track, offers some peace from the bustle of Kreuzberg. One would never suspect it was the site of some of the most consequential police violence in Berlin's post-war history. It all started on May Day — which had been celebrated in Berlin going all the way back to 1890.

On May 1, 1987, the West German government was trying to carry out a census. Many people objected to the state's attempt to register everyone. (Today, when people eagerly hand over all their data to private corporations, this might be hard to imagine.) A campaign to boycott the census was run out of an office in the Mehringhof in Kreuzberg (Gneisenaustr. 2a). Early in the morning of May 1, police stormed the building and confiscated campaign materials. Thus, the day began with political tension in Kreuzberg.

Like every year, leftists went to the traditional demonstration of the German Trade Union Confederation (DGB). These events, starting at 10 a.m., are full of beer, bratwurst, and bad music, and often led by Berlin's mayor (who tends to be a social democrat). Back then, autonomists and communists would form a "black-red block" that would push right up to the stage and shout slogans against the union bureaucrats. Those bureaucrats would get police to eject leftists from the demonstration.

With the union event over by noon, many radicals went home to Kreuzberg. That year, an internationalist street festival was taking place at Lausitzer Platz — similar to the union event, but with better politics, more lively music, and more varied food. Around the edges of the festival, there might have been a bit of shouting or shoving with cops — but nothing out of the ordinary for Kreuzberg in the 1980s. No one understood why the police attacked in force. At 7:30 p.m., they advanced onto the square with batons, water cannons, and tear gas. One teacher who was living on Lausitzer Platz in 1987 reported there was so much tear gas that they couldn't return to their apartment for three days!

But people fought back. And as the police withdrew, autonomists began breaking windows and plundering the surrounding shops. Again, nothing unusual for Kreuzberg. But this time, it wasn't just the usual suspects: More and more working-class families used the opportunity for "proletarian shopping." Everyone from small children to senior citizens joined in, and it became a real Kiezaufstand (Neighborhood Uprising). At least three dozen shops were plundered, with damage estimated up to 15 million marks.

By 10 p.m., the police were forced to retreat from the entire kiez — as telephone poles were knocked over and the neighborhood became pitch black, the "autonomous republic of Kreuzberg" was proclaimed. That might sound exaggerated, but it makes sense when we remember that we are talking about a tiny peninsula surrounded on three sides by the wall. For several hours, the police withdrew entirely to positions behind Görlitzer Bahnhof.

With a pirate radio reporting live from the area, people from across the city headed to SO 36. To prevent more insurrectionists from arriving, police shut down the two subway lines passing through Kreuzberg. Soon, the empty subway station Görlitzer Bahnhof was in flames. Cars were flipped over and lit ablaze to create barricades. The police only reentered around 2 a.m. It wasn't so much the cops that won the day — by the early hours of the morning, all the alcohol requisitioned from shops had made it impossible to hold the barricades.

6.6. Bolle Supermarket
Omar-Ibn-Al-Khattab-Moschee — Wiener Straße 1-6

The mosque at the corner of Wiener Straße has a Las Vegas chic. The Omar-Ibn-Al-Khattab-Moschee with all its marble and chandeliers opened in 2010. This was once the site of a chain supermarket called Bolle. During the Neighborhood Uprising in 1987, while many shops were plundered, this was the only one that burned to the ground. Its ruins stood here until 2004 — a kind of unofficial monument to the uprising.

In 2007, 30 years after the fire, the *taz* newspaper interviewed a pyromaniac who had been in prison for many years. By his own account, he had set 700 fires across Europe before he was arrested in 1990. He recalled that he had been in Kreuzberg on May 1 more or less by accident. After seeing molotov cocktails fly through the windows of Bolle, he thought: "That will never work!" So he took his own incendiary device and threw that in as well. It does kind of degrade the legend, but it's probably true.

Across the street from the mosque, at the corner of Man-teufelstraße (See Stop 9.8), the façade of an apartment building is covered with a colorful, hand-drawn political poster. The anonymous group Plakatief has been putting up a new left-wing message here every month since 2001. Their motto is, "18

The Bolle supermarket was burned to the ground. See Stop 6.6. Photograph copyright Mike Hughes / Umbruch Bildarchiv.

square meters of leftist activism." They reached the high point of their fame when they wrote about the National Socialist Underground, a Nazi terrorist group that killed nine immigrants in the 2000s. In response to ever-more revelations about links between the NSU and the secret services, the artists wrote "police and nazis — hand in hand." The cops came with a cherry picker to remove that — they felt they were being insulted. Since then, the posters are accompanied by a caption from the German constitution: "Censorship does not take place."

6.7. Revolutionary May Day
Oranienplatz

The Neighborhood Uprising was a jolt for revolutionary groups of all different stripes. The following year, they decided to hold their own demonstration in Kreuzberg. On May 1, 1988, at 1 p.m., 10,000 people gathered on Oranienplatz and marched down Oranienstraße. They were sporting the DIY look of West Berlin autonomists: leather jackets, ski masks known as Hasskappen (literally: hatred caps), and banners made of old bedsheets and spray paint. Besides autonomists, there were Stalinists, anarchists, Maoists, squatters... this was one of very few occasions when just about everyone on the radical left could come together.

Revolutionary May Day has taken place every year, in some form or another, for more than 30 years. A few times in the 1990s, the demonstration moved to Friedrichshain or Prenzlauer Berg (See Stop 9.4), and more recently it has gone through Neukölln — but Kreuzberg was always the natural habitat for revolutionary mobilizations. Each year, a huge demonstration would lead seamlessly into some kind of riot. Dumpsters and cars would burn as thousands of cops brought in from across Germany marauded through the kiez. Over the years, this has tended toward spectacle, with teenagers attempting to test their courage and tourists hoping to witness some violence.

Recounting all the ups and downs of those decades, which have included pitched fights between revolutionary groups, and even one murder, would require a whole chapter, or perhaps a one-hour documentary. (Fortunately, such a chapter exists in German in the guidebook *Rebellisches Berlin*, while a documentary was published in 2007 as *20 Jahre Revolutionärer 1. Mai*.) We will have to limit ourselves to just a few highlights.

1999 was the year of the NATO bombing campaign against Serbia — this was the first German war of aggression since 1945. Revolutionary May Day became the largest anti-war demonstration anywhere in Germany. At the time, the anti-globalization movement was slowly emerging, and the radical left was suddenly cool again. The Antifascist Action Berlin had ski-masked spokespersons on MTV inviting people to Kreuzberg. The band Atari Teenage Riot, which combined political credibility from the Friedrichshain squatting scene with enormous commercial success, headlined the demonstration. Standing atop a loudspeaker truck slowly moving down Kottbusser Damm, they played their hit "Start the Riot" — while an actual riot was circling around them! Michael Moore might have shot a music video with Rage Against the Machine leading a protest in front of the New York Stock Exchange, but he can eat his heart out.

On May 1, 2001 — this was right before the explosive mobilizations against the G8 summit in Genoa — the Berlin Senate decided to prohibit Revolutionary May Day altogether. This suspension of the right to assembly, with the uncomfortable memory of Bloody May Day in 1929 (See Stop 4.10), only served to bring more people onto the streets. That year, street battles between 10,000 demonstrators and thousands of cops moved up and down Oranienstraße, lasting all day and into the night.

My first Revolutionary May Day was in 2003, when the demonstration was directed against the Iraq War. May 1 was actually the day when George Bush put on a flight suit to declare "Mission Accomplished." In 2004, however, a new "left-wing" government in Berlin announced a new strategy. Rather than trying to ban the protests, they decided to fill the space with other people. This was the birth of MyFest (a pun on the German month of "Mai"). It was presented as an initiative by residents and shopkeepers to stop the annual violence.

Behind the scenes, however, it was financed by the police and the Senate. Over 100,000 drunken revelers now fill Kreuzberg on May 1. Some years, MyFest has been very effective at preventing demonstrators from forming a coherent mass. Other times, demonstrations have carved a path through the crowds and even drawn in new sympathizers. As darkness falls, the revelers inevitably start throwing bottles at cops. MyFest was never about preventing violence — it was about driving radical politics out of Kreuzberg.

As of this writing, Revolutionary May Day continues. There was a break in 2020 at the beginning of the Covid-19 pandemic — and even that year saw thousands of people illegally on the streets of Kreuzberg. The tradition came roaring back in 2021, when over 10,000 people met at Hermannplatz wearing red FFP2 masks. That year, the demonstration headed to Neukölln, where it was broken up by police after just 700 meters.

6.8. Christian Ströbele
Dresdener Straße 10

The Green Party has been the dominant political force in Kreuzberg for decades. The unassuming storefront in a building covered with bright-colored fish is the nexus of that power. For many years, this was the office of Christian Ströbele, Kreuzberg's representative in the Bundestag (the only directly elected Green MP in Germany). Since his retirement, the new MP is the similarly Green Canan Bayram.

Ströbele is a good symbol for how Kreuzberg has changed over the years, sliding from angry anti-capitalism to granola-fed "alternative" politics. Ströbele was a bit old for the 1968 movement, so he supported the movement as a defense lawyer. He joined the Social Democratic Party (SPD) as part of the "long march through the institutions," but was expelled in 1975. Ströbele had come to national prominence as a lawyer for members of the Red Army Faction (RAF), and a right-wing tabloid published a letter he wrote to his clients addressing them as "dear comrades." He maintains that this was not out of political sympathy for terrorism — "Genossen" is just what you called everyone back then.

Ströbele was later among the founders of the alternative daily newspaper *taz* in 1978. They campaigned in support of the left-wing guerrilla FMLN, collecting money for "Weapons for El Salvador." By 1992, a total 4.7 million marks had been donated. Ströbele filled a suitcase with cash and handed it over to an FMLN representative in Nicaragua. Being a good German, he asked for and got a receipt. In the mid-1980s, Ströbele also joined the new political party Alternative List, which eventually folded into the German Green Party.

It was the success of these projects that spelled their doom. The Alternative List joined the West Berlin government in 1989 — and before long, a party that had been founded by squatters was responsible for huge police operations to evict squats. (See Stop 7.11) When the Green Party joined the national government in 1998, the same thing happened: A party founded by pacifists and socialists ended up leading the first German war of aggression, as well as the biggest attacks on the welfare system, since 1945.

While the Greens and the *taz* newspaper have abandoned any semblance of left-wing principles, Ströbele has tried to stand his ground. He was one of the only Green MPs to vote against the war against Serbia, for example. Critics — and I would count myself among them — say he provides a lefty fig leaf for a thoroughly neoliberal and militaristic party. Then again, when he heard I was leading tours past his office and talking shit about him, he invited me inside for an interview. For many years, Strö-bele's unmistakable silver hair and red bicycle were a feature at every demonstration.

6.9. Refugee Camp
Oranienplatz

The tallest tree on this picturesque square, once part of the Luisenstadt Canal, is a plane tree (Platanus). Twenty-five years after the Neighborhood Uprising of 1987, a new protest tradition started on Oranienplatz. In 2012, refugees across Germany began demanding freedom of movement. While their asylum applications were being processed, they were forced to live in refugee centers. This could mean years stuck in the middle of nowhere, without access to public transport, jobs, or education — people were separated from their families or even anyone who spoke their language.

After a suicide in the city of Würzburg, refugees from Bavaria got organized. Openly defying the law that forbid them from leaving the county to which they had been assigned, in mid-2012 they began a protest march to Berlin. They travelled 600 kilometers by foot, arriving on October 6. Ten thousand people joined a demonstration to greet them. They then went to Oranienplatz and set up a protest camp. Rather than being trapped in the countryside, they wanted to be seen, right in the middle of the capital.

Before long, 200 people were living here — the square looked a lot like a refugee camp.

As the first winter set in, they additionally occupied an abandoned school down the road. (See Next Stop) There are so many people in Germany who lack papers and need a place to stay. Soon, 600 people were living in the school, while another 200 remained in the camp.

The city and district governments made numerous attempts to get rid of them — the conservative party CDU claimed that the refugees would cause a "plague." In April 2014, the Senate managed to convince a small number of refugees that they would get papers if they dismantled the camp. This was never a serious offer — but a handful of desperate people believed it. So one morning, these individuals came and started destroying the shacks with hammers and crowbars. One hundred other refugees were trying to stop them, as solidarity activists attempted to calm the situation. Police made no attempt to stop the fighting, but soon moved in to bulldoze the entire encampment. There were hundreds of witnesses, yet every single capitalist media outlet in Germany repeated the government's fake news: "Refugees leave camp voluntarily."

One particularly brave refugee named Napuli Langa, a woman from Sudan, broke through this lie. She climbed to the top of the plane tree and refused to come down unless the eviction was stopped. She threatened to jump if the police tried to remove her. Thus began a standoff: Napuli stayed atop the tree in the cool, wet April weather. The police shut down the entire square to prevent anyone from giving her food, water, or blankets. Now, at least, no one could claim the refugees had left voluntarily. After four days,

Napuli was partially successful: The tents were all removed, but the refugees were allowed to keep a shipping container on the square to share information about their struggle, and also a big circus tent to hold meetings. That tent was burnt down a year later, and now nothing remains. The Oranienplatz nonetheless remains a center of refugee protests.

6.10. Occupied School
former Gerhart-Hauptmann-Schule — Ohlauer Straße 22

This building was once a school. A few months after it closed, the empty building was taken over by refugees on December 8, 2012. Soon, up to 600 people were living in the former classrooms. The sanitary conditions were awful, with just a single shower for everyone, and this led to conflicts — one person was killed after a fight over the shower.

In mid-2014, a few months after the camp was destroyed, the government tried to use the same cynical playbook to evict the school. They wanted to claim that the refugees had decided to move out. Again, they promised that everyone who left would be placed in a shelter and have their asylum applications reviewed. When the police came, hundreds of refugees did get on the buses. Forty of them, however, inspired by Napuli's action in the tree, went to the roof. They said they would jump off if police entered the building. A new standoff began.

The local Green Party politicians called in the police, who promptly shut down a six-block area around the school. Only people with official addresses inside the "red zone" were allowed to cross the police barriers. This meant almost 100 businesses were cut off from customers. This police siege lasted for six days, with 40 people on the roof surrounded by thousands of heavily armed police. Thousands of school students went on strike, demonstrating right up to the police lines and proclaiming, "you can't evict a movement." Green Party offices across Germany were occupied. Eventually, the politicians blinked. The people on the roof — and only those 40 individuals — would be allowed to stay in the building.

But this was only temporary. The last people in the Gerhard-Hauptmann-Schule were evicted in 2018. Over the course of these evictions, 540 refugees were promised that their asylum applications would be reviewed. Of them, a total of three actually got residency permits.

6.11. Köpi
Köpenicker Straße 137

This decaying palace has been decorated by 10,000 bickering artists. My favorite touch is the green head from the Statue of Liberty, just like in the finale of *Planet of the Apes*. The Köpi is actually just the back half of a building with a courtyard — the front half was destroyed, but I've never figured out if that was due to the war or due to the wall. It was occupied in February 1990, just a few months after the wall came down. (We are no longer in Kreuzberg, but close enough.)

There were many squats in West Berlin, but even more in East Berlin. As the GDR focused on building new housing in places like Marzahn, hundreds of thousands of old apartments in the inner cities were left empty. When people broke open the doors and moved in, the authorities did not particularly mind — Stalinism had no need for evictions. Even Angela Merkel, when she moved to East Berlin, squatted an apartment in Mitte! After 1989, East Berlin saw a massive wave of political occupations. (See Stop 7.11) The Köpi, however, was the first joint East-West squat.

The Köpi mostly provides housing for lots of people, both in the building and in the surrounding caravans. But there are also spaces for concerts, workshops, movies, and political meetings. You can find public events on the calendar — Eastern European hardcore is a specialty — as long as you don't act like an annoying tourist.

In the early years, no one cared about this building — it wasn't worth much from a capitalist point of view. But as Kreuzberg and Friedrichshain gentrified, there was more interest in the plot of land near the river. In 2007, the land underneath the Köpi was sold to a private investor. Their plan was to tear down the house and build an office building. They began construction — standing in front of the Köpi today, you can see the now-abandoned concrete frame on the left.

There were protests all over the city — both in front of the Köpi and in front of the investor's office. If I am going to be honest here, I was not optimistic that the Köpi would survive for much longer. Then, something weird happened: The city caved in. They offered the investor a tax write-off in order to abandon their plans. That's why the construction site remains a shell and the Köpi remains full of life. Unfortunately, the half-finished construction now blocks a slogan that was once scrawled in huge letters: "The border doesn't run between peoples — it runs between above and below."

This is another case where we can only speculate about the secret deliberations of state actors. I think it has to do with the Ungdomshuset, the most important squat in Copenhagen. It was evicted in March 2007 to make way for some Christian cult. In the following days, tens of thousands of people took to the streets in some of the biggest riots Denmark had seen in decades. There were 690 arrests in three days — even the Little Mermaid statue was spray painted with an anarchy symbol! As a result, I think, Berlin politicians got cold feet. If dreamy Copenhagen saw such upheaval, what would happen in Kreuzberg?

In the years since the Köpi was saved, however, a number of important squats in Friedrichshain have been evicted, and realty speculators have become bolder. On October 15, 2021, 2,000 police officers in riot gear evacuated not the Köpi itself, but the caravan park next to the building. Police used pepper spray and armored vehicles to force their way in.

6.12. Gecekondu
Admiralstraße

It's not just squatters who have faced eviction in Kreuzberg. Let's return to our starting point at Kottbusser Tor. The traffic circle is almost entirely surrounded by a ring of concrete towers with colorful facades making them only slightly less dreary. On the southwest side of Kotti, the ground floor of one such tower is Berlin's premiere queer hangout, Südblock. In the summer, the square in front turns into the gayest of beer gardens.

The shack opposite, cobbled together out of old pieces of wood, is called Gecekondu. That's Turkish for an improvised settlement at the edge of a city — and this small house was indeed built without a permit or a plan. The apartment buildings went up between the 1950s and the 1970s with public subsidies. In exchange, rents were capped. But at the beginning of the millennium, much of Berlin's housing stock was privatized and thrown onto the open market. Within just ten years, rents in the city doubled. Families who had lived around Kotti for generations were forced to move out to the boondocks.

In 2012, residents of these buildings decided they needed to do something — anything. They set up a protest tent so neighbors could get to know each other. They planned to leave it there for a weekend. But an endless stream of people showed up — not just from Kotti, but people from all over the city, as rents were exploding everywhere. So the tent remained. Soon it was replaced by a bigger tent. And then by a shipping container. And now there is a real house.

The movement that these neighbors started, named Kotti&Co, has had some success in curbing the most exploitative rents. Beyond that, they helped renters realize that we are not alone — many Berliners are facing the same existential problems. This hut became a gathering point for a tenants' movement that mobilized tens of thousands of people. In 2018, Berlin got a Mietendeckel (rent cap) that lowered rents across the city. When that law was overturned by the Constitutional Court, it forced people to consider more radical options, such as the proposal to expropriate Berlin's biggest landlords. The campaign Deutsche Wohnnen & Co Enteignen (expropriate Deutsche Wohnen & Co., referring to the city's biggest realty company) was launched right here at the Gecekondu.

I once interviewed older residents who had moved into these buildings in the 1950s. They described the strange experience: For most of a lifetime spent in Kreuzberg, they were mocked relentlessly by West Berliners. The neighborhood was called "Little Istanbul" and the subway line U1 was the "Orient Express." They would sometimes even claim to live elsewhere — but at least it was cheap! Then all of a sudden, rich people started constructing new buildings next door with car elevators. From one day to the next, the once denigrated neighborhood was the place to be.

Kreuzberg is going to remain a site of struggles. Its central location on the banks of the Spree is too much for speculators to resist. With the MediaSpree initiative, the opposite banks in Friedrichshain — once home to great clubs in industrial ruins — are filling up with corporate gray goo. There are shopping malls, office towers for giant tech companies, and a Mercedes-Benz Arena — boring monuments to neoliberalism that look like they were ordered from a catalogue. Kreuzberg even got its first McDonalds! And while the focus of the radical left might have switched somewhat south to Neukölln, Kreuzberg is going to remain an angry neighborhood fighting back against these changes.

Vladimir Ilyich Ulyanov at Lenin Square in East Berlin. See Stop 7.4.
Photograph copyright Umbruch Bildarchiv.

The East Is Red

7.1. House of the Ministries
former Reichsluftfahrtministerium — former Haus der
Ministerien — Detlev-Rohwedder-Haus (Finance Ministry) —
Wilhelmstraße 97

This colossus with long windows set in grey stone is designed
to make us tremble before the power of the German state. It was
built for the Hermann Göring's Reich Ministry of Aviation in
1936. But just a decade later, it was repurposed for a radically
different government attempting to dismantle the Nazis' legacy.

"Risen from ruins," the anthem starts, "and facing the future."
The German Democratic Republic (GDR), more commonly
known as East Germany, was founded on October 7, 1949.
Göring's former haunt was renamed the House of the Ministries.

After the war, Stalin had wanted Germany to be a neutral capitalist country, like Austria or Finland. But the imperialist powers
could not accept this — they needed a militarized Germany as
a buffer against the Soviet bloc. So they introduced a separate
currency in the French, British, and American occupation zones
in mid-1948, as the first step toward the foundation of the (capitalist) Federal Republic. This forced the Stalinists to found their
own Democratic Republic in the Soviet zone — though Stalin

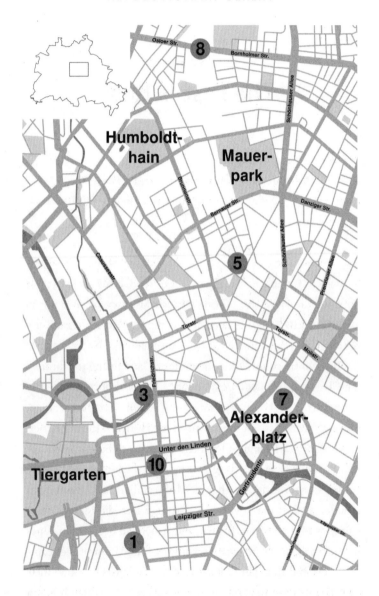

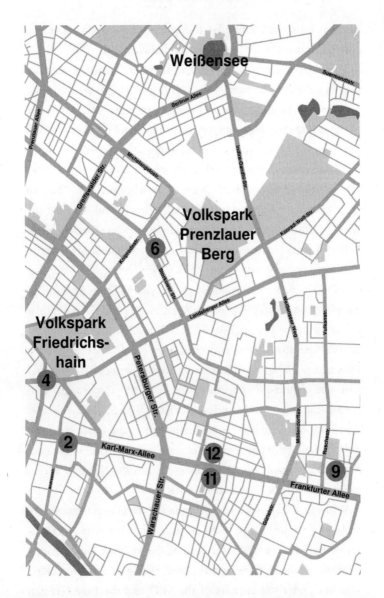

made at least one more offer to liquidate the socialist state if a united Germany would only remain demilitarized.

Was either German state democratic? Every bourgeois democracy is ultimately a sham — in Marx's words, it means nothing more than "deciding once in three or six years which member of the ruling class [is] to misrepresent the people in Parliament." Yet even by the standards of the bourgeoisie, the "democratic" republic in East Germany with its People's Chamber was a farce. "It has to look democratic," Walter Ulbricht once said, "but we must keep everything in our hands." Ulbricht had once led the KPD's Berlin-Brandenburg District (See Stop 4.12) and returned to Berlin from Soviet exile as Stalin's man to set up a new system.

The Socialist Unity Party (SED) was created by merging the KPD with a small rump of pro-Soviet SPD members. The founding congress took place on April 21, 1946, in the Admiralspalast theater at Friedrichstraße 101. The KPD was represented by Wilhelm Pieck, who had once been a collaborator of Rosa Luxemburg. The most prominent social democrat they could find was a third-rate bureaucrat named Otto Grotewohl, who later became the GDR's prime minister. The Stalinists also set up additional parties — a christian-democratic party, a liberal party, a nationalist party, and a peasants' party — that were under the SED's control. All these parties formed the National Front, which regularly won 99% in elections.

When East Berlin workers protested against the government in mid-1953, they marched to the House of the Ministries. An uninspired Stalinist mural on the side of the building shows happy workers, farmers, intellectuals, and young people marching together under the banners of the SED and the Free German

Youth (FDJ). This marked quite a contrast to the angry workers on the street demanding free elections. Now an image of the demonstrations in 1953 is sunk into the square, just beneath the mural.

Today, the building is called the Detlev-Rohwedder-Haus and it is the seat of Germany's finance ministry. Wolfgang Schäuble, who led the EU's offensive to subjugate Greece in the early 2010s, had his office here, in Göring's building. German imperialism barely tries to hide its continuities.

7.2. Stalinallee
Karl-Marx-Allee 70e

As soon as the self-described workers' and peasants' state was founded, the GDR began the work of reconstructing the capital. On December 21, 1949, Berlin's old Frankfurter Straße was renamed Stalinallee in honor of the 70th birthday of the Soviet dictator. A 4.8-meter / 16-foot bronze statue of the "Man of Steel" was installed in 1951. The statue stood next to a fountain in the shape of three squares in front of Karl-Marx-Allee 70e — today a sign marks the spot.

East Germany's National Construction Plan, launched in 1952, called for "workers' palaces" on both sides of Stalinallee. These apartment blocks in the wedding-cake style of Stalinist baroque tower over both sides of the broad avenue. The street has been used in the Netflix show *The Queen's Gambit* to represent Moscow in the early 1960s.

When Stalin died in 1953, a new Soviet leadership began to criticize the worst aspects of the cult of personality. Under Walter

Ulbricht, the GDR also went through a process of slow and recalcitrant De-Stalinization. In the early morning of November 14, 1961, all the street signs on Stalinallee were replaced and the statue was taken down. People went to sleep in one street and woke up in a different one — an official announcement only followed several days later. The front part of the street became Karl-Marx-Allee and the back part was called Frankfurter Allee. It was much more complicated in Stalinstadt, a city built from scratch on the GDR's border with Poland. It was renamed Eisenhüttenstadt.

Construction workers were told to break the Stalin statue into tiny pieces. A few bits disappeared into the pockets of their overalls. As a result, Stalin's ear and half of his mustache can still be seen at Café Sibylle at Karl-Marx-Allee 72. Most of the bronze was melted down and used to cast statues for the East Berlin Zoo. Remnants of Stalin now form part of the saber-tooth tiger and the elk there — alongside the bronze lions that were expropriated from a statue of Kaiser Wilhelm. (See Stop 10.2)

Around the same time, the "workers' palaces" proved far too expensive for a bombed-out country that desperately needed housing. Instead, the GDR built Plattenbauten, buildings made out of prefabricated concrete. The avenue became an architectural hodgepodge. Starting in the 1960s, new construction in the Karl-Marx-Allee had a modernist look, including treasures like Café Moscow and the Kino International cinema.

The GDR's economy lacked many things — it was famously difficult to get oranges and bananas — but the government did provide housing for everyone at a very low cost. Capitalist Germany today, with far greater resources, leaves hundreds of thousands of people without homes.

7.3. Bertolt Brecht
Theater am Schiffbauerdamm — Bertolt-Brecht-Platz 1

The Theater am Schiffbauerdamm with its proud turret stands just off the Spree river. The playwright Bertolt Brecht and the composer Kurt Weill debuted their most famous work, the *Three-Penny Opera*, here in 1928. The opening song *Mack the Knife* was written right before the premiere after the lead actor demanded a bigger role. Brecht created numerous plays in an epic style intended to teach the audience revolutionary values, including *The Mother* and *Saint Joan of the Stockyards*.

Brecht fled Germany after the Reichstag fire in late February 1933. He settled in Scandinavia before eventually traveling via the Soviet Union to California. He was able to outwit the House Un-American Activities Committee in 1947, but returned to Europe the next day. Denied entry into West Germany, he eventually moved to East Berlin. In 1949, Brecht and his partner, the actress Helene Weigel, founded the Berliner Ensemble at the Theater am Schiffbauerdamm. They lived just down the road at Chausseestraße 125.

Brecht was a communist, but an independent one.

In May 1953, the SED decided to increase the "norms," the work quotas, by 10%. This was a de facto wage cut. It was construction workers on Stalinallee who held a first protest in the Rose Garden at Karl-Marx-Allee 102–103 on June 16. They marched toward the headquarters of the trade union federation, gathering workers from other construction sites. When the union leaders refused to speak to them, they continued to the House of Ministries. The SED's Politburo quickly cancelled the increase of the norms, but by now the 10,000 demonstrators were demanding the resignation of the government and for free elections. They called for a general strike.

The following day, June 17, protests took place in 7,000 cities and towns across the GDR. Up to a million people· went on strike, cheered on by the American radio station RIAS. Protesters occupied police stations, SED offices, and prisons. The GDR leadership offered concessions — but also denounced the protestors as "provocateurs and fascist agents." The Soviet military, with half a million soldiers in the GDR, declared a state of emergency and sent tanks into the streets. At least 17 people were killed in East Berlin during the uprising, and over 2,000 were arrested.

Bourgeois historiography presents June 17 as a "German uprising" demanding reunification with the capitalist West. Like other revolts in Stalinist states, such as Hungary in 1956 or Czechoslovakia in 1968, it was a complex and contradictory movement. Western secret services were certainly looking for opportunities to destabilize the planned economy — but in no way were the masses calling for the reintroduction of capitalism. Quite the opposite: In April 1946, 78% of people in Saxony had voted for the nationalization of businesses belonging to "war criminals and Nazis" — which was pretty much the entire bourgeoisie. Many demonstrators in 1953 waved German flags, but this was not to show support for West Germany, as is often falsely claimed. The GDR used the exact same flag until 1959 — only then did they add their emblem with hammer, wreath, and compass.

After the protests, Kurt Barthel, an author and SED official, chastised the construction workers. He warned them they would have to "lay a lot of bricks and act very wisely before this disgrace can be forgotten."

Brecht responded with a poem: "After the uprising of the 17th of June / The Secretary of the Writers' Union / Had leaflets distributed on the Stalinallee / Stating that the people / Had forfeited the confidence of the government / And could only win it back / By increased work quotas. / Would it not in that case be simpler / for the government / To dissolve the people / And elect another?"

Brecht died in 1956 and Weigel in 1970. Both are buried in the Dorotheenstadt Cemetery next to their home. Many of Brecht's plays can still be seen at the Berliner Ensemble. Yet the traditions of epic theater have been lost — it is rare to see audience members interrupt the shows to discuss the political lessons with the actors.

7.4. Lenin Square
former Leninplatz — Platz der Vereinten Nationen

Stalin disappeared from East Berlin in 1961, almost as mysteriously as the countless communist oppositionists he had made disappear. This left more room for Vladimir Ilyich Ulyanov, better known as Lenin. For his 100th birthday on April 22, 1970, a 19-meter / 62-foot statue made of red granite was unveiled in Friedrichshain. This was the center of Leninplatz, the starting point for Leninallee. Today, the square is a simple affair with apartment towers on three sides, just south of Volkspark Friedrichshain.

The statue was demolished in 1991, despite extensive protests by Lenin's neighbors. The dismantling was dramatized in the 2003 film *Good Bye, Lenin!* — although no helicopter was used in real life. The granite blocks were buried in a sandpit near the Müggelsee lake. Twenty-five years later, Lenin's massive bald head was dug up again and put on display in the Spandau Citadel. Now it can be seen, laid on its side, alongside a smorgasbord of Wilhelmine statues that once lined an avenue through the Tiergarten park (where a memorial to the Red Army is now located).

Lenin Square was sadistically renamed United Nations Square, and Lenin Avenue became Landsberger Allee. All over East Berlin, street names were changed in the early 1990s, often returning to aristocratic traditions. Dimitroffstraße, named after the Bulgarian communist Georgi Dimitrov, is now Danziger Straße. Hermann-Duncker-Straße, named after a collaborator of Rosa Luxemburg, became Treskowallee, honoring an aristocratic house — that street goes past the former seat of the Treskows, now the East Berlin Zoo. (See Stop 10.2) Even Clara-Zetkin-Straße was renamed in 1995! (See Stop 9.3)

There was no real system for distinguishing "good" from "bad" communists. Karl Liebknecht kept his street next to Alexanderplatz. August Bebel, on the other hand, the head of the SPD who died in 1913 and can therefore hardly be accused of Stalinist sympathies (See Stop 8.1), lost a school in Prenzlauer Berg, which now bears the name of John Lennon.

Lenin Square had the largest Lenin monument in East Berlin, but it was far from the only one. Another stood in the foyer of the House of Soviet Science and Culture at Friedrichstraße 176–179. The building remains open as the Russian House —

Lenin, unfortunately, disappeared without explanation. At least one Lenin statue is still standing today: The moving company Zapf Umzüge has one standing at its headquarters at Nobelstraße 66 in the industrial area past the canal at the very end of Neukölln. It was acquired by the company's owner, the eccentric leftist capitalist Klaus Zapf, in the dissolving Soviet Union. The library at the Humboldt University's Faculty of Law at Bebelplatz 1 has two stained-glass windows of Lenin. The building once housed the Royal Library, where Lenin studied works by Marx and Engels during a visit to Berlin in 1895. He also took part in a workers' meeting in Friedrichshain, and a metal plaque marks the spot at Frankfurter Allee 102.

Lenin was treated as a kind of secular saint in East Germany. But were his ideas put into practice? In *State and Revolution*, Lenin had argued that with the advance of socialism, the "special apparatus for coercion called the state" would become unnecessary and wither away. With the increasing self-organization by working people, he wrote, "the need for a special machine of suppression will begin to disappear." After 40 years of the GDR, with its enormous wall and complex system of surveillance, could anyone claim the state was "withering away"?

7.5. Zion Church
Zionskirche — Zionskirchplatz

Zion Church stands atop Weinbergsweg — a road going up a hill where a vineyard once stood. The protestant church was opened in 1873 with a donation from Kaiser Wilhelm. Dietrich Bonhoeffer, a pastor who went on to lead Christian opposition to the Nazis, worked here in the early 1930s.

In East Germany, the SED crushed any kind of civil society. The regime's most dogged opponents left for the West — around 4 million people "voted with their feet" over the GDR's 40-year history. Many who stayed and tried to protest were charged with "anti-state agitation." That is why there was not much of a 1968 movement in East Berlin, for example. When GDR citizens tried to protest against the invasion of Czechoslovakia in front of the Soviet embassy on Unter den Linden, they were all arrested within minutes. At least 1,000 people were arrested over the summer for expressing solidarity with the Prague Spring. A single graffito with the name of the Czech reform communist Dubček has been preserved on the back wall of the State Library, opposite Dorotheenstraße 28.

Inside the churches, however, a certain opposition was tolerated. The GDR allowed Germany's two main churches to operate autonomously — but it also provided alternatives to religion. Instead of protestant confirmation, for example, 13- and 14-year-olds in East Germany could do a secular "youth consecration" — a tradition that continues to this day. While the Federal Republic subsidizes both state churches, protestant and catholic, with billions of euros each year, the Democratic Republic separated church and state. As a result, if East Germany were still a country today, it would be among the world's most atheistic countries.

After the Chernobyl disaster in 1986, activists set up an Environmental Library in the basement of Zion Church. They printed a newspaper called *Umweltblätter* (Environmental Newspaper) — it was declared a religious publication, and therefore it could be legally distributed inside East German churches. This kind of activism was direly needed behind the Iron Curtain. The GDR had a formal commitment to protecting nature — it even had an environmental minister starting in 1971, more than 15 years before the West did — but its ecological practices were devastating.

One year after the Environmental Library was founded, the Ministry of State Security (Stasi) searched the church basement, arrested the activists, and confiscated the printing press. There were public protests — not just in Western countries, but also with a candlelight vigil in front of Zion Church. The government caved in, releasing the detainees and returning the press. This gave the *Umweltblätter* and the whole East German opposition a big push.

On October 17, 1986, a rock concert took place in Zion Church. Two thousand young people crammed into the nave to see bands from both halves of the city. West Berlin was represented by Element of Crime (whose singer went on to write the novel *Herr Lehmann / Berlin Blues*). East Berlin sent Die Firma (whose guitarist later joined Rammstein). The bands played right next to the altar — the event was officially a "worship service with music."

At the end of the concert, 30–40 Nazi skinheads attacked the crowd, shouting "Sieg heil!" and "No Jews in German churches." The People's Police were present but did nothing to stop the fascists. According to official ideology, the existence of a right-wing youth subculture under socialism was simply impossible. The authorities initially tried to downplay the attack as apolitical hooliganism. After the events were reported in the Western media, however, the GDR put the Nazis on trial and sent several to prison. One leading skinhead turned out to be the son of a Stasi officer — a major who was responsible for observing "right-wing extremism," no less.

Today, East Germany has been swept by far-right sentiment, with the racist party Alternative for Germany (AfD) getting 25% or more in regional elections. Bourgeois intellectuals try to blame this on the legacy of the GDR, as right-wing tendencies there were deliberately ignored. This theory seems absurd. There was ultimately only a tiny fascist movement in East Germany. It was the 30 years *after* the restoration of capitalism that turned militant racism into a mass phenomenon. Under the Federal Republic, Nazis were no longer ignored — now, the domestic secret service offered financial and political support to violent fascists.

7.6. Church from Below
Kirche von Unten — Storkower Str. 119

Every year, the protestant churches of the GDR gathered for an Evangelical Church Assembly. In 1987, church leaders wanted it to take place in East Berlin, as part of the celebrations for the 750th anniversary of the city's founding. They entered into negotiations with the SED and agreed to clamp down on oppositional activities inside the churches.

Rank-and-file church groups felt the official event was too close to the government, so they held their own Church Assembly from Below. It took place from June 24–26, 1987, in the Pentecost Church at Petersburger Platz 5. Six thousand people attended discussions and concerts, and additional rooms had to be used in the nearby Galilee Church at Rigaer Straße 9. Participants called for "Glasnost in the State and the Church," referring to the opening taking place in the Soviet Union under Mikhail Gorbachev. They also demanded a "Social Peace Service," as young men in the GDR who did not want to perform the obligatory military service were still required to do an "Alternative Military Service" that supported the army.

After the event, the Church from Below became a permanent network, taking over rooms in the Elisabeth Church at Invalidenstraße 4a. This space was used for punk concerts, but also for opposition meetings. On May 7, 1989, local elections were held across East Germany. According to the official results, almost 99% had voted for the National Front. Voters could simply fold their ballots to show support for the only list — voting against it required going into a voting booth, which was noted by officials. The election law mandated that the vote count be public. For the first time in the GDR's history, activists attempted to check the results. In polling place after polling place, they counted more "No" votes than appeared in the final tallies. These findings were tabulated in churches across East Germany, revealing systematic fraud. This was a watershed moment in the GDR's terminal crisis.

After reunification, the Church from Below continued as a youth center for punks. For years they were located at Kremmener Straße 9 near the Mauerpark, but they had to move in 2014. They found a new home in a low building covered with graffiti at Storkower Straße 119 in Lichtenberg, just outside the S-Bahn Ring. At a benefit gig for a socialist youth group, I asked one of the social workers why this not particularly Christian-looking club was called a "church." He said that the youth center had once been in a space with a vaulted ceiling that looked like a "church from below." I'm still not sure whether he was joking — maybe enough time has passed that the origins of the name have been forgotten.

7.7. Alexander Square
Alexanderplatz

Alexander Square retains much of its late Stalinist architectural charm. The area around the Red City Hall was once full of narrow streets — the square was named for Tsar Alexander I when he visited Berlin in 1805. Beginning in the late 1950s, the neighborhood was rebuilt with an open layout as an example of socialist urban planning. When it was completed in 1971, Alexanderplatz became the center of East Berlin. The Fernsehturm (TV tower), the Fountain of Friendship Between Peoples, and the World Time Clock were all completed in 1970–71. Three decades of capitalist development has placed a Starbucks in the tower's base, but not ruined the square's vibe.

As the year 1989 progressed, East Germany began to crumble. Under Gorbachev, the Soviet government made clear that democratic reforms were needed in the GDR, and subsidies would be cut. In the case of unrest, Soviet tanks could not be counted on to protect the SED government like in 1953. Meanwhile, GDR citizens began traveling to Hungary and crossing the border to Austria in order to reach the West.

October 7 was the 40th anniversary of the GDR's founding. The National People's Army paraded down Karl-Marx-Allee.

The night before, 75,000 members of the Free German Youth (FDJ) had marched through the city center carrying torches. Foreign guests came from around the world, including Gorbachev, Nikolai Ceausescu from Romania, Wojciech Jaruzelski from Poland, Daniel Ortega from Nicaragua, and Yassir Arafat from Palestine.

It was simultaneously the five-month anniversary of the fraudulent local elections. Demonstrators gathered near the Palace of the Republic, chanting "Gorbi" for the Soviet leader, and threatened to disrupt the official celebrations inside. Only when Gorbachev's plane had departed did the police begin to attack demonstrators, arresting 1,200. Police repression in the GDR was usually able to break up protests before they had been seen — but this was happening at a massive scale, and most of the country saw it via Western TV.

State violence only inspired more protests. On October 29, the head of the SED in Berlin, Günter Schabowski, invited citizens to a discussion with "open doors and open words." Around 20,000 people gathered in front of the Red City Hall, asking questions about the repression of October 7 and about the myriad problems of daily life in East Germany. Under pressure from the crowd, SED officials were forced to concede that further demonstrations would be allowed.

That is how the GDR saw its first-ever legal demonstration not organized by the regime. On November 4, 1989, up to 300,000 people gathered at Alexanderplatz. A hand-drawn poster was stuck on the State Council Building: "Pluralism instead of Party Monarchy!" — so much dissent had never been seen in East Germany. Artists and activists gave speeches, as did GDR politicians who saw which way the wind was blowing. Schabowski of the SED and even Markus Wolf, the recently retired head of the Stasi's Main Directorate for Reconnaissance (foreign secret service), called for changes.

But it would be wrong to assume that the masses were demanding capitalism. The author Stefan Heym (who had fled Germany in 1933, returned as a soldier of the U.S. Army in 1943, and later protested against the post-war rehabilitation of Nazi elites, which convinced him to move to the GDR) gave words to the feeling:

> It is as if someone has opened a window after all the years of stagnation, of intellectual, economic, political stagnation, years of stifling and stale air, of phrase mongering and bureaucratic arbitrariness, of official blindness and deafness. The socialism that we want to finally build — the real one, not the Stalinist one — for our benefit and for that of all of Germany, this socialism cannot be conceived without democracy.

7.8. Border Crossing
Bösebrücke

An iron bridge leads over the train tracks, above garden parcels on either side. The Bösebrücke (which literally means the Bridge of Evil, though it's actually named after the communist resistance fighter Wilhelm Böse) connects Wedding in the West to Pankow in the East. This unspectacular spot at Bornholmer Straße is where the GDR got its death blow.

As disturbances grew across East Germany, the SED's leaders realized they had to let steam out of the boiler. On the afternoon of November 9, the SED's Politburo and Central Committee decided that GDR citizens would now be allowed to travel outside the country. This would require a passport (which few people owned) and a visa — each document would take weeks to acquire. The calculation was that protesters would be assuaged by hearing that they could cross the border in just a few months' time.

The decision was to be announced by Günther Schabowski at a press conference at 6 p.m. At the GDR's International Press Center at Anton-Wilhelm-Amo-Straße 37 (the building now belongs to Germany's Ministry of Justice and Consumer Protection), Schabowkski explained that GDR citizens could now leave "at all of the GDR's border crossings to the FRG," including in Berlin. Reading from a piece of paper he had gotten from the SED's new leader Egon Krenz, he did not notice that the text was only to be published the following morning.

When a reporter asked when the new travel regulations would go into effect. Schabowkski replied with the political gaffe of the century: "As far as I know..." he said, "it is effective immediately... without delay." Within an hour, the statement was on West German TV and thus seen by most of East Germany. Many people did not begin compiling paperwork — instead, they went right to the nearest border crossing.

At first, a few dozen people gathered in front of the checkpoint at Bornholmer Straße. Then it was a few hundred. By the evening, several thousand were demanding to leave. The border soldiers had no idea what to do — they had heard the announcement on TV just like everyone else. They called their superiors, but no one dared to issue orders. Starting at 9 p.m., individuals were allowed to pass through the checkpoint, but the crowd kept growing. Border guards were trained to shoot to kill anyone deemed a "deserter of the republic" — but not this many at once. At 11:30 p.m., the officer in charge raised the barrier, and thousands of East Berliners streamed across the Böse Bridge. By midnight, other border crossings opened as well.

Twenty-eight years after it had been built, the wall was effectively gone. It had been brought down by the same principle behind every strike and every demonstration: They can't stop all of us! The air was full of energy — this was a chance to restart socialism. All such hope was crushed over the next year, as East Germany was swallowed up by its capitalist neighbor.

7.9. Stasi Headquarters
Stasi-Museum — Nonnenstraße 20

The nondescript buildings facing Frankfurter Allee are surprisingly easy to overlook — they were designed that way. Heading toward U-Bhf Magdalenenstraße, there is a brownish office tower on the corner, followed by a row of what look like small apartment buildings. Only by passing between them do we see that this is all part of a massive complex filling two city blocks.

This was the headquarters of the Ministry for State Security, which considered itself "the second best secret service [in the world] after the Mossad." Up to 20,000 agents worked in the 29 buildings here. They saw themselves as the "shield and sword of the party," modeled after the Cheka, the Soviet secret police founded by Felix Dzerzhinsky. The Stasi, as it was popularly known, was both a domestic and a foreign secret service. In the East, the Stasi observed anyone suspected of oppositional thought. In the West, the Stasi placed agents everywhere, including in the FRG chancellery in Bonn and the NATO headquarters in Brussels. Many of these agents only had their cover blown years after the GDR collapsed.

The Stasi had 91,000 full-time employees and almost 200,000 informants — this in a country with just 16 million inhabitants. This is, when you think about it, the most damning fact about East German Stalinism: The country's brightest minds could have dedicated themselves to culture, science, or making life more comfortable. Instead, they spent inconceivable resources persecuting young people who listened to Iron Maiden and observing other "threats to socialism."

Just nine days after the wall fell, the Stasi was renamed the Agency for National Security. All over the GDR, regional Stasi offices were occupied by demonstrators. The headquarters, however, continued to function. On January 15, 1990, 100,000 people gathered in front of the complex and broke in via a gate on Ruschestraße. Stasi agents had been shredding their mountains of files, and civil rights activists wanted to preserve them.

As an author, I have a double conflict of interest here. I would not have thrived in the GDR. The Stasi arrested people like me — the Trotskyist Oskar Hippe spent almost ten years in an East German prison. Even trying to acquire a copy of Trotsky's book *The Revolution Betrayed* was a criminal offense. But today there is an entire industry explaining how bad East Germany was. Shouldn't someone point out that the GDR was also supporting the Namibian independence struggle against the South African Apartheid regime? (See Stop 1.7)

I also have fond memories of Peter Wolter, who was my first boss when I started working in journalism. He spent years at international news agencies, eventually leading Reuters's London bureau. Only after the wall came down was it revealed that he had been working for the Stasi since 1973. Peter never got a cent from them, which is part of the reason that Stasi agents were so hard to detect. Why did he sign up? "I wanted to prevent a world war," he said. Peter and I had a fun work relationship. "What's the deal with that American Trotskyist?" he would ask people around the office. "He must have contacts to the CIA!" I'm pretty sure he was joking.

Building 1 of the Stasi HQ was the seat of Erich Mielke, who headed the agency from 1957 until 1989. Today it houses the Stasi Museum. Mielke's office is preserved, as is the "casino" next door where people could relax after conferences. The casino originally included men's and women's bathrooms — but the latter was turned into a small kitchen after they realized that there were never any women present at meetings of Stasi leaders. This was another contradiction of the GDR: Free childcare and full employment led to unprecedented freedom for women — yet leadership roles remained almost entirely male.

7.10. *House of Democracy*
former Haus der Demokratie — Friedrichstraße 165

This grand building on the most tourist-filled part of Friedrichstraße has a Hugo Boss store, a gourmet food shop, and some doctors' offices. Opposite is the Westin Grand Hotel, which the GDR opened in 1987 to serve foreign tourists. Not too many neo-

Gothic buildings with carved stone façades survived in central Berlin, but here there are three in a row. This corner is where the GDR was wrapped up.

After the wall came down, the future of East Germany was completely open. That year, the Polish United Workers Party had formed a "round table" with the oppositional union Solidarnosc. Following this model, representatives of the East German regime sat down with new political parties and social movements at a "round table" — which was actually square-shaped — at Schönhausen Palace in Pankow, the GDR's official guest house.

New political formations sprouted up across the country — most were copies of West German parties. There was a CDU, an SPD, and a liberal party. The SED renamed itself the Party of Democratic Socialism (PDS). An independent socialist party called itself the United Left. Different opposition groups formed Alliance 90 — it fused with the Greens in 1993, and the Green Party is still officially called Alliance 90/The Greens. They all agreed to hold new elections to the People's Chamber on March 18, 1990.

All these new parties needed office space. Gregor Gysi of the SED-PDS offered the headquarters of his party's district leadership in Berlin-Mitte at Friedrichstraße 165. The GDR's Council of Ministers decreed that all parties would receive office equipment and even two automobiles each. They moved into the rechristened House of Democracy on January 10, 1990. The elections were surprisingly democratic, with even the smallest groups allowed to appear on the ballot and on TV. East Germans re-founded both a Communist Party (KPD) and an Independent Social Democratic Party (USPD), but these remained tiny.

Trotskyists coming in from the West formed a Spartacist Workers Party and a League of Socialist Workers, which were even tinier.

In 1999, the House of Democracy was forced to leave Mitte, moving to Greifswalder Straße 4 in Prenzlauer Berg, close to Volkspark Friedrichshain. The new building, called the House of Democracy and Human Rights, provides space for dozens of NGOs.

7.11. Battle of Mainzer Straße
Mainzer Straße

After the wall came down, East Berlin experienced a brief moment of freedom — more than the GDR had ever offered, but also more than capitalist Germany would ever tolerate. With the planned economy in rapid dissolution, huge swaths of the city were owned by everyone and no one.

The old tenement apartments on Mainzer Straße in Friedrichshain, south of Frankfurter Allee and U-Bhf Samariterstraße, were scheduled for demolition. Instead, at the end of April 1990, they were all occupied simultaneously, in a joint action by autonomists from the West and oppositionists from the East, including the Church from Below. Thirteen of the street's 28 apartment buildings were taken over, with each offering space for a different community. Mainzer Straße 3 was for women and lesbians, while Mainzer Straße 4 was for gay men, a replacement for the Tuntenhaus that had been evicted in 1983. (See Stop 8.8)

Mainzer Straße existed in relative peace for half a year, but conflicts began around November 12 — just a month after reunification on October 3. Police began evicting other buildings in

East Berlin, and squatters responded with demonstrations. The cops attacked Mainzer Straße 9 believing an autonomist command center was located inside, but they were forced to retreat.

As the situation escalated, the occupiers built massive barricades across both ends of Mainzer Straße — they even expropriated a backhoe to dig out trenches. They simultaneously offered to remove the barricades and open negotiations if the government would promise not to evict them.

Instead, on November 13, Berlin's social democratic interior senator ordered the biggest police operation in Berlin's post-war history. Backed up by ten water cannons and multiple helicopters, 3,000 officers assaulted the block. Fearing projectiles from above, they first occupied the roofs and then pushed down into the buildings. The street was defended by about 500 autonomists with rocks and molotov cocktails. The fighting lasted two hours and ended with 417 arrests.

As the dust settled, Mainzer Straße looked like a war zone. Representatives of the public housing company that owned the buildings said they had never requested an eviction. The Alternative List (AL), who formed the government together with the SPD, said they had never been informed about the operation. The social democrats countered that a sudden attack had been necessary due to squatters' "violent criminality" — and that the AL had indeed participated in the decision.

On November 16, the AL left the government in protest, ending the term of Berlin mayor Walter Momper. A coalition government collapsed after one party had ordered a violent eviction in secret — there was a weak echo of the Bloody Christmas of 1918. (See Stop 2.8) The AL later merged into the Green

The squatters of Mainzer Straße put up barricades to defend their homes from police. See stop 7.11. Photograph copyright Umbruch Bildarchiv.

Party. This episode was typical of the Greens' later development. Many Green Party politicians had once been squatters themselves, but by 1991, they were responsible for unprecedented violence against the squatting scene.

After reunification, up to 130 buildings in East Berlin were occupied. Over the course of the 1990s, some were evicted, and others were legalized. By the 2000s, Berlin no longer had any truly occupied buildings, with all that remained enjoying some form of precarious legality. Today, Mainzer Straße has been completely gentrified and nothing reminds visitors of the Battle of Mainzer Straße.

7.12. Silvio Meier
Silvio-Meier-Straße — U-Bhf Samariterstraße

Silvio Meier moved to East Berlin in 1986, at age 19. He joined the punk scene, as well as the Environmental Library and the Church from Below. (See Stops 7.5 and 7.6) He was one of the organizers of the punk concert on October 17, 1986, that was attacked by Nazis. Meier's older brother had fled to West Berlin, and he established contact to the band Element of Crime. Those musicians travelled to the East as tourists, without permission to perform, and had to borrow instruments from their hosts.

As soon as the wall came down, Meier became active in the squatters' movement, and helped occupy the building at Schreinerstraße 47 in Friedrichshain. Schreina47 remains occupied to this day.

On November 21, 1992, Meier was hanging out with friends. They ran into a group of eight Nazis on the street and there was a melee. Meier was able to rip a patch off a Nazi's jacket that said, "I am proud to be a German." The two groups met other again at U-Bhf Samariterstraße, and there was another fight. On the landing on the Western side of the station, one of the Nazis pulled a knife and stabbed Meier several times. He died from the wounds — he was 27.

A plaque marks the spot where Meier died, with an antifascist oath: "No forgiving, no forgetting!" A street was supposed to be dedicated to Meier on the 20th anniversary of his death, but due to legal wrangling, the name Silvio-Meier-Straße was only unveiled in 2013. For almost 30 years, thousands of young people have gathered at Samariterstraße every year for a Silvio Meier Demonstration. In black hoodies and sunglasses, waving flags and lighting flares, they march through Friedrichshain chanting antifascist slogans.

Rigaer Straße is currently the center of Berlin's militant squatting scene, but the neighborhood is rapidly gentrifying. The "red-red-green" government has destroyed a number of house projects: Liebigstraße 11 was evicted in February 2011; Liebigstraße 34 was cleared out in October 2020, almost 30 years after it was first occupied. As I write these lines, the squat at Rigaer Straße 94 is acutely threatened.

*   *   *

On October 3, 1990, the German Democratic Republic was annexed by its Western neighbor. East Germany's industry was destroyed, and millions of people lost not only their jobs, but also their identities. East Germans won the freedom to travel, if they can afford to — but now they are equally "free" to live under a bridge. The ban on abortion — which the GDR had lifted in 1972 — went back into effect and remains in place today. (See Stop 9.11) West Germany's secret services, run by fanatical right wingers, built up neo-Nazi organizations across the East. Due to widespread joblessness, the German army now recruits half of its soldiers in the East. From there they are sent to commit murder in Afghanistan, Mali, and other countries — this is capitalism's much vaunted "freedom to travel." The GDR leaves behind some general ideas about what is possible under socialism, such as universal employment, a right to housing, and free childcare. But it equally shows how Stalinist bureaucracy, obsessed with control and repression, makes it impossible to realize that potential.

Charlotte von Mahlsdorf in the Gründerzeitmuseum she founded. See Stop 8.9. Photograph copyright Monika Uelze / Gründerzeitmuseum.

8

Queer Berlin

8.1. August Bebel
Habsburgerstraße 5

This off-white facade has a towering entrance, though it is still slightly less impressive than its neighbors. Near the heart of today's rainbow neighborhood, this was once the home of Germany's most well-known socialist — and an early advocate for gay rights.

August Bebel, the co-chair and central leader of the Social Democratic Party of Germany (SPD), lived here. Bebel was a member of the Reichstag from 1867 until his death in 1913, with a few interruptions while he was in prison for insulting the Kaiser. Bebel spent the last decades of his life at different addresses in Schöneberg, then outside of Berlin, not far from other socialists living a comfortable bourgeois lifestyle. (See Stop 3.3)

In 1879, Bebel published the massive book *Woman and Socialism*. With lots of historical data spread over more than 500 pages, he argued against the institution of marriage and for the socialization of housework, showing how socialism would lead to the complete emancipation of women and all oppressed people. 52 editions of the book appeared in Bebel's lifetime, and it was translated into 20 languages — the most influential socialist book in Germany at the time, far outselling anything by Karl Marx.

When the German Empire adopted its criminal code in 1871, Paragraph 175 prohibited homosexual acts between men (as well as sex with animals). Women having sex with other women were not included in the ban, as the all-male legislators could not picture what that would even look like.

In 1897, a group called the Scientific-Humanitarian Committee drafted a petition against Paragraph 175, and it eventually gained 6,000 signatures. The elderly leader of the SPD was among the first signers, and on January 13, 1898, Bebel took to the floor of the Reichstag to speak out. Bebel argued that a ban was impossible to enforce:

> The number of these [gay] persons is so great and reaches so far into all levels of society, that if the police here scrupulously carried out their duty, the Prussian State would immediately be compelled to build two new penitentiaries just to take care of those offenses against Paragraph 175 that are committed in Berlin alone.

Be gay, do crime! Bebel, the prominent feminist, also demanded that women be included equally in any law. The speech was pragmatic, and nothing like a burning defense of queer liberation that we would expect from a socialist politician today. But a socialist was nonetheless the first politician in the world to speak out for the decriminalization of homosexuality.

Bebel lived in this building when he gave the speech in 1898. He later lived at Hauptstraße 97, where a plaque is dedicated to him. That apartment building has lost all its former elegance as a result of chaotic post-war additions including discount art deco cladding.

Bebel's plea had no effect: Paragraph 175 remained on the books in Germany for another 120 years. The number was so consistent that it became a code for queer people to identify each other. A personal ad would say "1.75 meters tall," or someone would ask "were you born on May 17?" (which is rendered in German as "17.5."). In Weimar times, communists and social-ists pushed to abolish the law — but they could not get a majority before the parliament itself was abolished. After power was handed over to the Nazis, they made the law much more repres-sive, criminalizing even minor forms of same-sex affection, and increasing the maximum sentence to five years in prison.

After the war, Paragraph 175 survived in different ways. Just weeks after the Nazis' unconditional surrender, Berlin cops had returned to harassing gay men. East Germany revoked the Nazis' version of the law, yet maintained the Weimar version — sup-posedly to protect "workers' morals." In the 1950s, however, the German Democratic Republic effectively decriminalized con-sensual homosexual acts. Yet queer people still faced systematic discrimination, and even modest attempts at political organizing were blocked with the full force of the Stasi. (See Stops 8.9 and 8.10) The East German law was finally abolished in 1988.

West Germany, in contrast, kept the Nazi version of Paragraph 175 — the constitutional court explicitly supported Hitler's law in 1957. As one historian remarked in 1963: "For homosex-uals, the Third Reich has not yet ended." By the time the law was reformed in 1969, 100,000 men in the Federal Republic of Germany had been investigated and 50,000 convicted. There were even cases of gay men who survived the concentration camps — and after the war were put on trial again for the same

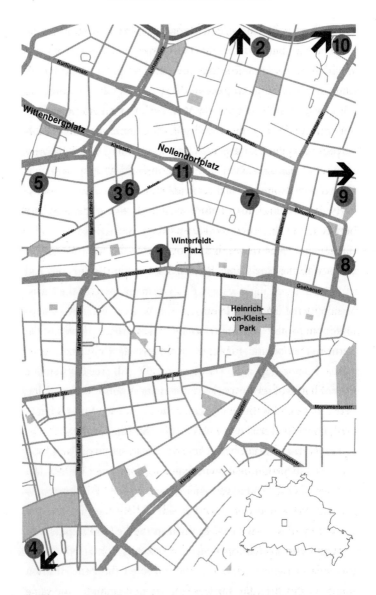

"crime"! In some cases, it was the exact same judge (now no longer a Nazi but a "democrat") who pronounced that a gay man would have to serve a full sentence, since time in a concentration camp did not count as prison time.

In 1969, West Germany reformed the law, yet homosexual acts with men under 21 remained illegal, meaning that a different age of consent applied to gay men. It was only in 1994 that a now reunited Germany completely decriminalized homosexuality. Convictions from the Nazi era were annulled in 2002. Astoundingly, it took until 2017 before most men who were convicted between 1945 and 1969 received pardons. We should remember that number when we see right-wing parties like the CDU waving rainbow flags at the official Pride demonstrations.

8.2. *Institute for Sexual Research*
Memorial for the Institut für Sexualwissenschaft — banks of the Spree river, next to the Haus der Kulturen der Welt

On the banks of the Spree river, not far from the new chancellery in the shape of a washing machine, stands West Berlin's Congress Hall, now called the House of World Cultures. There is a terrace to eat pizza and drink beer while tourist boats float by. A bit to the west, an ugly brown metal box marks the site of a villa that once stood at the end of the old Beethovenstraße. (To be precise, the villa was actually on the other side of the congress hall, but I guess they thought it would look better on the riverbank.)

Magnus Hirschfeld opened the Institute for Sex Research in this villa in 1919. He had previously led the Scientific-Humanitarian Committee, the world's first organization advocating for the rights of homosexual and transgender people. Hirschfeld first became interested in sexuality and gender while helping patients who struggled with shame relating to their desires — too many of them were driven to suicide. The persecution of Oscar Wilde in London in 1895 inspired Hirschfeld to take action.

Hirschfeld began interviewing gay men and also visiting "human zoos" to speak with people from German colonies about sex in their cultures. (See Stop 1.8) He became famous across Germany with the petition against Paragraph 175, but even more so when he testified in a scandalous trial. A Prussian general was suing a reporter over an article about a gay affair between the officer and a friend of the Kaiser. Hirschfeld argued for the defense that the general was clearly gay, and there was nothing wrong with that. He hoped to gain acceptance for homosexuality by showing that some of the most prestigious men in the Empire were gay. His testimony, however, had the opposite effect, and made him — a queer Jew — an object of hatred for völkisch nationalists. Hirschfeld's praise for the French Revolution of 1793 for decriminalizing homosexuality led to even more accusations of being un-German. In 1919, Hirschfeld worked on the film *Anders als die Anderen* ("Different from the Others") — the first-ever sympathetic depiction of gay men on screen. It ended with a dramatic appeal against suicide.

In 1919, Hirschfeld opened his institute in a villa in Tiergarten. It offered medical consultations, educational lectures, and an enormous archive of scientific and pornographic material. Doctors there even performed the first gender-affirming surgery for a trans woman named Dora Richter. Hirschfeld lived at the institute and welcomed revolutionary thinkers like Walter Benjamin and Ernst Bloch.

This had all been possible because the social democratic government in the German state of Prussia declined to enforce Paragraph 175. When that government was toppled in an institutional coup in mid-1932, police harassment of gay men in Berlin increased, yet the institute was able to remain open. On May 6, 1933, Nazi students stormed the building. The SA arrived later and stole all the books — many of which were included in the state-sponsored book burning four days later. Before the Nazis had come to power, Hirschfeld had left for an international lecture tour, and remained in exile. He died in France in 1935.

In 2008, a Memorial to Homosexuals Persecuted Under Nazism was set up in the Tiergarten, just opposite the Memorial to the

Nazis destroy the library of the Institute for Sexual Research on May 6, 1933. See Stop 8.2. Photographer unknown. Via Wikimedia Commons.

Murdered Jews of Europe — less than two kilometers from where Hirschfeld's institute once stood. The metal column containing a looped video has been controversial among queer people: Should lesbians be included alongside gay men? Did lesbians suffer the same kind of murderous persecution under fascism?

8.3. Eldorado
Biomarkt Speisekammer Eldorado — Motzstraße 24

Life for queer people in 1920s Berlin was, of course, not just about research and activism. Magnus Hirschfeld was also a fixture on the gay scene, where he was known as Aunt Magnesia. Up to 300 clubs for homosexuals were opened in different parts of the city, with as many as 100 operating at any one time. One of the most famous ones was at the center of what today remains Berlin's rainbow neighborhood.

The first location of Eldorado opened at Martin-Luther-Straße 14–18 in 1926. A second was launched two years later just a block down at Motzstraße 24. Clubs like these were known as "transvestite locales," featuring same-sex dancing and drag shows. It was hard to tell who was a man and who was a woman, or if it even mattered. Marlene Dietrich performed at elaborate balls at Eldorado, and author Christopher Isherwood came here frequently (he lived just around the corner at Nollendorfstraße 17).

In mid-1932, with Prussia under the control of a right-wing German government, the Berlin police launched a "comprehensive campaign against Berlin's vice-filled nightlife" to stop "dance revelries of the homosexual kind." The clubs faced increased harassment, but remained open. In the year after the

Nazis came to power, all such spaces were shut down for good. Eldorado was handed over to the Nazis' paramilitary SA. In place of the old motto — "Here it's OK!" — the entrance was covered in swastika flags.

The Nazis, despite their violent hostility to homosexuality, attracted a number of gay men to their ranks. The SA chief of staff Ernst Röhm was a regular at Eldorado and other queer clubs. After he was publicly outed in 1931, Röhm made no secret of his sexual orientation, even inviting journalists along for a night out. Eventually, in 1934, Adolf Hitler had Röhm killed — his SA was perceived as too rowdy and "revolutionary" — and only then did the Nazis scandalize his gay identity.

The building that housed Eldorado was — thanks to the consistently amusing dialectic of history — the place where Berlin's first post-war gay liberation group was founded. (See Stop 8.6) Today, an organic supermarket called Speisekammer (Pantry) has taken its place — how the neighborhood has changed! The sign "Eldorado" remains.

8.4. Wilhelm Reich
Schlangenbader Straße 12

He looks like a 1920s version of David Lynch: Wilhelm Reich had a stern visage topped by a shock of white hair. He was a doctor who became interested in psychoanalysis and sexuality at the University of Vienna. Reich was not the only person to attempt a synthesis between Marxism and psychology, but he was certainly the most influential. His greatest popularity, however, came after his death, as the 1968 generation began talking about "sexual liberation," a term Reich had coined.

Reich moved to Berlin in 1930 to join the Communist Party of Germany (KPD). He founded the Sexpol movement (full name: the German Society for Proletarian Sexual Politics) to offer sexual education, counseling, and contraceptives to the working class. The goal was revolutionary sexuality in the full sense of the term: If workers could toss off the chains of sexual repression, so the theory went, they would be more willing to fight for political and economic liberation as well.

Reich, at least in the 1930s, did not see sexuality as all-powerful. He defended the Marxist idea that social being determines consciousness. Reich's goal as a Marxist psychologist was to study the process by which a person's position in class society is translated into individual beliefs. Such a scientific undertaking was intended to help a revolutionary party awaken the masses' desire to struggle.

In 1933, Reich received a rare honor: He was expelled from the Stalinized Communist Party as a petty bourgeois psychoanalyst — and simultaneously expelled from the Psychoanalytical Association for being a communist! He remained in limited contact with dissident communists such as the exiled Leon Trotsky.

Reich's most influential book, *The Mass Psychology of Fascism*, was completed in early 1933. It had to be published in Denmark, as by that time Reich's works were being thrown onto Nazi bonfires. Reich argued that fascism's appeal to sectors of the masses — especially the petty bourgeoisie — was based on the authoritarian nuclear family and on sexual repression. Could it be any coincidence that the Nazi salute was so ostentatiously phallic? Or that their symbol, the "twisted cross," had been used throughout history as a fertility symbol, as it clearly shows two bodies intertwined in coitus?

He called for the abolition of Paragraph 175, but as was common among Freudians, Reich viewed same-sex attraction as a neurosis to be cured through treatment. Some on the left, especially among the Stalinists, saw fascist movements as homoerotic "men's leagues" and argued that homosexuality was inherently rightist, as if all fascists were gay or all gays were fascists. In the mid-1930s, Stalin's Soviet Union recriminalized homosexuality, turning back the sexual freedom of the October Revolution.

In exile in the United States, Reich went on a post-Marxist trip and began searching for the life force of the universe: magic particles he called "orgones." I would prefer not to get into that. I will close by pointing out that Reich lived on Berlin's Schlangenbader Straße, which literally means Snake Bath Street, with all the horrifically erotic undertones of that image. Reich believed that "every psychic experience (no matter how meaningless it appears to be) ... has a function and a 'meaning.'" I wonder what he would have to say about the address he chose.

8.5. It Is Not the Homosexual Who Is Perverse...
former Kino Arsenal — Welserstraße 25

This apartment building now has a large kiosk on the ground floor. There was once a small movie theater with 175 seats here, going all the way back to the earliest days of cinema in 1912. Kino Arsenal opened its doors in 1970 as an arthouse cinema with a focus on films from the Third World and socialist countries.

On August 15, 1971, the director Rosa von Praunheim showed a film that had premiered a month earlier at the Berlinale film festival. It's not clear how the title fit onto the marquee: *It Is Not the Homosexual Who Is Perverse, But the Society in Which He Lives*. The experimental film shows Daniel, a young gay man, moving to West Berlin and attempting to live with a partner according to the rules of bourgeois marriage. He soon breaks off this relationship and moves through the city's gay subculture, visiting bars, beaches, parks, and public toilets. In the spirit of a Brechtian Lehrstück (learning-play), the main character and the audience both learn that gay men can only be emancipated if they live openly and organize politically.

The film makes its lessons explicit in a rousing final speech, in the style of the play *Saint Joan of the Stockyards* (or perhaps an episode of *South Park*): "Be proud of your homosexuality! Out of the toilets and onto the streets! Freedom for the gays!" ("Out of the toilets" referred to sex in public restrooms but was also an attempt to translate "the closet" into German, as most German homes do not have built-in closets.)

This film was possible because of the reform of Paragraph 175 two years earlier — homosexual acts with men over 21 were no longer crimes. Some scenes were filmed around Nollendorfplatz, including a famous on-screen kiss shot at Bülowstraße 29. It was the first gay kiss in German film history, and lasted a full 45 seconds.

The screening was followed by a lively discussion with director Rosa von Praunheim and screenwriter Martin Dannecker (a sexologist whose script was inspired by his research). One participant recalls a speech about a utopia where all gay men would move to an island and create a Gay Republic. One of the few women in the audience called out: "But a gay capitalist is still an exploiter!"

Forty to fifty people in the audience decided to take up the film's call for political organization. They met again in the same theater two weeks later, and soon set out to create a new gay liberation group (See Next Stop). As the movie toured around West Germany, over 50 such groups were founded — an example of art inspiring action at a level that most attempts at epic theater could only dream of.

In 2000, Kino Arsenal moved into the basement of the new Sony Center at Potsdamer Platz. The old location remained a theater for a while, showing pornographic films until 2007.

8.6. Homosexual Action West Berlin
former Hand Drugstore — Biomarkt Speisekammer Eldorado — Motzstraße 24

Those gay men held a few more meetings at Kino Arsenal. Soon they needed a better space to draft a founding statement for their group, and they found one at Motzstraße 24. This was where Eldorado had been forced to close almost 40 years previously. (See Stop 8.3) In April 1971, a youth center called Hand Drugstore opened in the corner building — as the name suggested, it was for young people dealing with addiction. Activists from this youth center later occupied a floor in an office building at Potsdamer Straße 180 — that space, called Drugstore, was a center of Berlin's punk scene for almost 50 years until it was evicted in 2019.

The Homosexual Action West Berlin (HAW) was founded on November 21, 1971. Many of the 40 or so original members were also active in other groups from across the spectrum of the West Berlin left, including Stalinists, Maoists, and Trotskyists. Their goal was to liberate homosexuals alongside the working class. Rosa von Praunheim offered space in his studio at Dennewitz-straße 33 for the new group to organize. (The original building was torn down by 1973 to make way for a planned Autobahn right through the middle of West Berlin. This nightmare was, blessedly, stopped by protests.)

The HAW followed the call to go "out of the toilets." On May 1, 1972, they organized a Gay Block at the trade union demonstration. Later that month, they held their first national meeting over the Pentecost weekend. (The term "Pentecost Meeting" does not sound so strange in a German context — many socialist groups make use of the long weekend for organizing.) In 1973, 500 people from across West Germany came to the following Pentecost Meeting, which included a demonstration and a "kiss-in" on Kurfürstendamm. Some of the gay demonstrators wore hoods, identifying themselves with signs as a "teacher," "judge," "preacher," etc.

Like many of the gay liberation groups emerging around the world in the early 1970s, the HAW was both radical and broad, creating space for intense ideological debates. A so-called "Tun-tenstreit" (roughly: fag fight) about strategies for gay liberation began with the question of whether gay men should wear men's or women's clothes at demonstrations. One side (the "political faction") wanted to win equal rights in existing society as part of the class struggle — the other side (the "fun faction") wanted to challenge all gender roles. Meanwhile, representatives of the gay movement were slowly being coopted by capitalist society.

Around 1973, the HAW started a women's group, which took over a floor in the new headquarters at an old factory building at Kulmer Straße 20a. This group later became the Lesbian Action Center (LAZ). The HAW had passed its zenith by 1977, and formally dissolved in 1999. But over its lifespan, the group launched SchwuZ (Schwules Zentrum or Gay Center) as Berlin's first openly gay club. After a number of moves through the city, SchwuZ continues to this day, now in the old Kindl brewery at Rollbergstraße 26 in Neukölln. SchwuZ is where Berlin's first Pride parade in 1979 was planned. (In German-speaking central Europe, Pride is called Christopher Street Day, similarly commemorating the uprising that began at the Stonewall Inn at Christopher Street in Greenwich Village.) The first year, 400 people took to the street to "make your gayness public." The event has since grown to almost a million participants.

8.7. Prince Valiant
former Prinz Eisenherz Bookstore — Bülowstraße 17

The last time I checked, the storefront in this red-pink apartment building with the lovely turret on one corner was empty. On November 12, 1978, a full year before West Berlin's first Pride parade, a gay bookstore opened its doors here. Prinz Eisenherz is a figure from Nordic myths, and also the German translation of the 1950s comic strip *Prince Valiant*. The Prinz Eisenherz bookshop was one of the many cooperative businesses founded in West Berlin at the time.

The store was so successful that in the 1980s, it moved to Savignyplatz, which was the center of West Berlin's book market. (See Stop 5.7) Prinz Eisenherz became the biggest gay bookstore in the world. More recently, it has moved to smaller quarters at Motzstraße 23. As it is now for customers of all genders, it has dropped the Prinz from its name, becoming just Eisenherz.

Since 1993, Motzstraße has been home to a Lesbian-Gay Street Festival that attracts up to half a million people. The event, always balancing between the leather scene and family entertainment, has no radical tradition. It was launched by queer capitalists and the cops in order to promote rainbow capitalism. All the political parties — including the right-wing ones responsible for horrific persecution of gays — show up to wave rainbow flags. I saw a podium discussion at the festival in 2018 where every single politician called for increased funding for police — this would supposedly protect queer communities from violence and hate. One wonders how Berlin activists of the 1920s or the 1970s would feel about the idea that cops protect queer people…

At the festival, even the Israeli embassy has a stand. Israel's government relies on this kind of pinkwashing to cover up more than 50 years of occupation. We are told that wealthy gay men in Tel Aviv enjoy great freedoms — and are supposed to forget about the fates of Palestinian queers living under military administration and Apartheid. This pinkwashing campaign dominates the bourgeois gay movement in Germany. The Israeli ambassador, representative of a virulently homophobic right-wing government, was even invited to speak at the Pride parade in 2016. When queers from both Israel and Palestine tried to protest against him, they were physically attacked by German politicians. Apparently, beating Jews is how the German establishment proposes to "fight antisemitism."

Berlin's demographics are changing, however. The left and queer scenes used to be made up of white Germans convinced that it was not possible to criticize Israeli occupation. Now, the city is full of young activists from all over the world. As a result, there are more "Queers for Palestine" and anti-colonial slogans at Pride marches. After 50 years of co-optation, adaptation, and shifts to the right, Berlin's queer scene is rediscovering its radical roots.

8.8. Fag House
former Tuntenhaus — Bülowstraße 55

West Berlin's squatting scene was centered in Kreuzberg. (See Stop 6.1) But empty buildings in Schöneberg were also occupied. Bülowstraße 55 is a relatively new building — to the right, you can see older neighbors in the style of what used to stand here a century ago.

A few doors down, at Bülowstraße 57, Berlin's most famous lesbian café opened in 1921. The Dorian Gray was named after a book by Oscar Wilde. It offered space for music and dancing, but also for editorial meetings of *Frauenliebe* (Women's Love), the most important lesbian magazine in the Weimar Republic. The café was closed by the Nazis in 1933.

On February 12, 1981, the building at Bülowstraße 55 was occupied by ten gay men and a straight woman, who called their new home Tuntenhaus (roughly: fag house). They spent the next six months renovating the abandoned building in the middle of the rainbow neighborhood. Gay men from West Germany visiting the front-line city could crash here.

In 1981, West Berlin got a new conservative government that promised a hard line against squatters. On September 21, the police attacked eight different occupied buildings, and the interior senator personally inspected a squat at Bülowstraße 89. Demonstrators gathered in front of that building, and police shoved them down the road. The 19-year-old Klaus-Jürgen Rattay was forced onto the street at Potsdamer Straße 127, where he was run over by a bus and killed. This repression was largely successful: The squatters' morale was broken, and many people no longer believed they would be allowed to stay in their new homes. The Tutenhaus was evicted at the end of 1983 and the building was torn down.

When the wall came down in late 1989, there were new opportunities for people to take over empty urban spaces. Activists occupied all of Mainzer Straße in Friedrichshain at the end of April 1990. One of those buildings was taken over by about 30 gay men, and Tuntenhaus #2 was born at Mainzer Straße 4. The second "fag house" was evicted in the Battle of Mainzer Straße six months later. (See Stop 7.11)

The inhabitants then occupied the back building at Kastanienallee 86 in Prenzlauer Berg. It is hard to picture today, but Prenzl'Berg was a hotbed of squatters and radicals until the late 1990s. This became Tuntenhaus #3. Today, it remains as one of the last impediments to the neighborhood's gentrification. The occupants once had rental contracts with public housing companies, but the building was privatized and there have been long legal struggles against eviction. Big white letters on the facade describe the problem: "Capitalism normalizes, destroys, kills."

8.9. *Charlotte von Mahlsdorf*

Gründerzeitmuseum im Gutshaus Mahlsdorf — Hultschiner Damm 333

This late baroque, apricot-colored manor is not where you would expect to find a center of Berlin's queer movement. In fact, this far out in the East — in Mahlsdorf, on the outer edge of Marzahn-Hellersdorf, pushing against the border with Brandenburg — it might be hard to find anything progressive.

Mahlsdorf Manor was built in 1815 — over the centuries, it housed different bourgeois owners, and also an orphanage. But by the late 1950s, it was empty, and the local government planned to demolish it — why pour resources into restoring old aristocratic palaces when workers needed housing? That was the thinking in East Berlin, at least.

The manor was saved by Berlin's most famous trans woman, Charlotte von Mahlsdorf. She moved into the dilapidated building in 1958. She had previously lived in Friedrichsfelde Palace from 1946–8, similarly protecting it from demolition, decay, and looting. The surrounding park was transformed into the East Berlin Zoo in 1955, and the palace was for a time used to house chimpanzees. Now the palace in the middle of a zoo hosts classical music concerts. (See Stop 10.2)

Charlotte von Mahlsdorf was born in 1928 as Lothar Berfelde. The village of Mahlsdorf had just been incorporated into Greater Berlin. Even as a small child, she was always interested in girls' clothes and "old junk." As a teenager, she got a job with an antiques dealer clearing out old apartments, and kept interesting tidbits for herself. Her father, a violent man and a fanatical

Nazi, pushed her to join the Hitler Youth. When he threatened to murder her, her siblings, and her mother with his revolver, she took a massive wooden ladle and killed her father in his sleep. She was sentenced to four years in juvenile prison, but was released when Berlin was conquered by the Red Army. After the war, she worked as a museum curator and antiques dealer, saving old furniture from bombed-out homes. She also began to dress in a more proudly feminine style, eventually becoming Charlotte von Mahlsdorf.

She put her collection, including lots of grandfather clocks and gramophones, on display at Mahlsdorf Manor. This eventually became a museum dedicated to the ornate furniture of the Gründerzeit, the period of rapid economic expansion after the foundation of the German Empire in 1871, lasting until roughly 1900. She even managed to save Berlin's last traditional bar, located on Mulackstraße in the Scheunenviertel, the poor Eastern Jewish quarter north of Alexanderplatz. When the bar Mulackritze was torn down in 1963, she saved all its furniture and rebuilt it in the manor's basement.

Starting in 1974, this basement bar served as a meeting point for the Homosexual Interest Group Berlin (HIB). This was a safe spot for queers from East Berlin to gather. Charlotte von Mahlsdorf was able to fend off government attempts to nationalize the growing museum. In 1989, she had a cameo in East Germany's first gay film, *Coming Out*. That film premiered at Kino International on November 9 — the wall was opened during the premiere.

In 1991, the manor was attacked by Neo-Nazis — German reunification led to a wave of right-wing violence and terror. Charlotte von Mahlsdorf was granted Germany's Order of

Merit, but she felt she could no longer stay in the country. She emigrated to Sweden in 1995 and died on a visit to Berlin in 2002. The Gründerzeit Museum was taken over by an association and remains open today.

8.10. Sunday Club
Sonntags-Club — Veteranenstraße 26

East Berlin's Homosexual Interest Group (HIB) was founded on January 15, 1973, inspired by their counterparts in West Berlin. One of their first actions was at the World Festival of Students and Youth in 1973. (See Stop 9.10) Peter Tatchell from London was a member of Gay Liberation Front, and he joined the British Labour Party's delegation. He brought thousands of leaflets in English and German, which caused difficulties at both the West and East German borders. He was there alongside gay comrades from both West and East Berlin.

Homosexuality had been decriminalized in East Germany — yet political organizing by queer people (or anyone else) was prohibited. Tatchell had painted a sign for the festival's closing rally: "Homosexual liberation! Revolutionary Homosexuals Support Socialism!" Officials from the Free German Youth (FDJ) and their friends from the British Stalinist party tried to prevent the message from getting out, leading to numerous scuffles.

And this was the treatment meted out to visitors from the West! In East Berlin, the HIB was not allowed to register as an association, which meant it could not print leaflets or rent spaces for meetings. As was the case with many GDR oppositionists, queers had to hide under the umbrella of the protestant churches, where they founded Homosexuality Working Groups. Queer activists were constantly observed by the Stasi, while the authorities rejected all their proposals to create a homosexual communication center. The Stalinists argued with a Catch-22: There was no discrimination under socialism; therefore, any attempt to discuss the discrimination of homosexuals was by definition anti-socialist. Blocked from any kind of public activism, the HIB disbanded in 1980. It was only in 1987 that the SED and the FDJ slowly began to accept homosexuality.

Ursula Sillge had founded the HIB's lesbian group and relaunched it a few years after the HIB dissolved. Starting in 1986, they held meetings in the youth center Mittzwangiger-Club (Mid-Twenties Club) at Veteranenstraße 26 near Zionskirchplatz. The space was only free on Sundays, so the queer gatherings were soon called the Sunday Club. That location shut down in 1987, but the Sunday get-togethers continued in different restaurants and youth centers — the neutral-sounding name helped avoid attention.

The Sonntags-Club filed their paperwork to register as an association on November 12, 1989 — just three days after the wall came down. They were recognized on July 7 of the following year, becoming the first officially recognized, independent group for lesbian, gay, and bisexual people in the GDR. Throughout the 1990s, the association developed new activities: youth work, AIDS support, a trans group, and more. Today, the Sonntags-Club is housed in a former library at Greifenhagener Straße 28, just outside the S-Bahn ring.

Gay men in East Berlin didn't just need space to organize. The lowest part of Volkspark Friedrichshain, on the Western tip, contains the Märchenbrunnen: a Fairytale Fountain surrounded by statues from the Brothers Grimm stories, including Hansel and Gretel, Snow White, Sleeping Beauty, and Puss in Boots. When it was built at the beginning of the twentieth century, this "popular" art led to extended conflicts with the Kaiser, while it was a huge hit among the working class. In the 1980s, this became the biggest cruising spot in East Berlin. Surrounding areas of the park have that function today, as the fountain area is now closed at night.

8.11. Rainbow Neighborhood
Nollendorfplatz

This elevated train station — one of Berlin's oldest above-ground stations — is topped with rainbow neon lights. Nollendorfplatz has been the heart of Berlin's queer scene for more than a century.

In 1989, a stone plaque was put on the side of the station for the queer victims of fascism — the first one in Germany. It contains two words in German — "beaten to death, silenced to death" — on a pink triangle, which was the symbol gay men were forced to wear in the concentration camps. Of the 10,000 gay men sent to the camps, less than half returned. Lesbians were not covered by Paragraph 175, but they were also persecuted under fascism as so-called "asocials," and they were forced to wear black triangles.

Today, Berlin has a reputation for being a queer capital, having finally abandoned the many terrible forms of persecution that marked the entire twentieth century. Berlin elected its first openly gay mayor in 2001, with the social democrat Klaus

Wowereit coming out just before the vote: "I'm gay, and that's a good thing!"

A small number of white gay men have been allowed to enter the ranks of the bourgeoisie. Germany has had a gay vice chancellor (Guido Westerwelle from the neoliberal FDP) and a gay health minister (Jens Spahn from the conservative CDU). A leader of the far right is a lesbian (Alice Weidel from the AfD). It is hard to ignore that these four prominent gay politicians have all defended social cuts and racist policies. This fact shows that there is only one kind of "liberation" that capitalism offers to queer people: consumption of rainbow-colored products, while a handful of queers get the opportunity to become exploiters and oppressors themselves. Meanwhile, the masses of queer people suffer from both precarious living conditions and ongoing forms of oppression. Christopher Street Day (CSD) has turned into an enormous party, but one that is dominated by corporations, cops, and conservative politicians.

The last 50 years show that class remains central to queer liberation. The goal of Berlin's old-school queer movement was gay liberation as part of the liberation of the working class and the oppressed. Since 1998, there have been anti-capitalist Pride marches in Berlin as an alternative to the conformist CSD, with names like "Transgenial CSD." These have been marked by ruptures and plenty of left infighting. But as I write these lines, Berlin just held its first internationalist, anti-colonial, and pro-Palestinian Pride march. This is a first step to make Pride a riot again.

The Women's Center on Hornstraße in Kreuzberg. See stop 9.6. Photograph copyright Margarete Redl-von Peinen.

Berlinerinnen

9.1. Moabit Unrest
Sickingenstraße 20-23

This sleepy industrial park next to the train tracks is full of small businesses whose purpose is hard to decipher. In 1910, the biggest riots of Berlin's inter-revolution period (between 1848 and 1918, that is) took place in this street. A street battle lasting several days and involving tens of thousands of people started with a simple labor dispute.

On September 19, 1910, 136 coalmen went on strike. They delivered coal to homes and businesses for Kupfer & Co., a small company belonging to the industrial baron Hugo Stinnes. With the cost of living rising quickly, the workers demanded a wage increase from 43 to 50 pfennig per hour. Management refused to negotiate, and scabs drove out the coal wagons under the protection of mounted police. Within days, professional strikebreakers, some armed with pistols, arrived. Strikers went out at night to dig up the cobblestone streets.

Solidarity in the working-class district of Moabit was enormous. Industrial workers from nearby factories went on solidarity strikes. Young women broke the windows of shops that served strikebreakers. Police drew their sabers and attacked the crowds, who responded with rocks and bottles. Stinnes person-

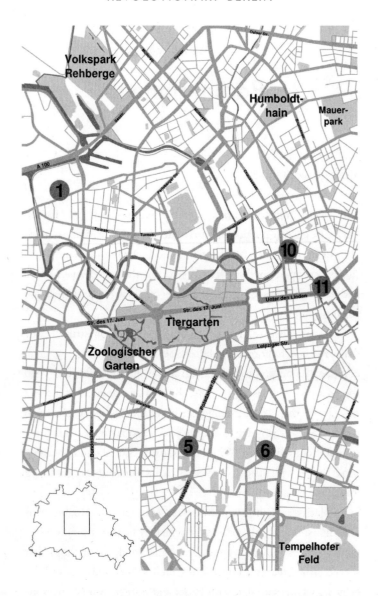

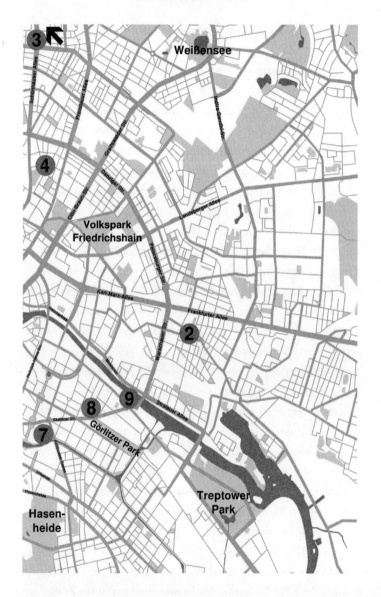

241

ally called on the Prussian interior minister to intervene, and he sent a total of 1,000 police officers.

Ten days after the strike began, police estimated that 20,000 or 30,000 workers were out on the streets — one out of every seven people in Moabit! Reports in the international press described militant actions by women as one of the "alarming signs of revolution." British journalists noted that "shrieking women, with babies in their arms, made their way to the fighting line or raved like bloodthirsty amazons through the streets." Another dispatch noted the "excesses committed by young girls and also by the worst class of Berlin females." (Klaus Thelewelt's psychoanalytical study *Male Phantasies* looks at this right-wing obsession with women as agents of revolutionary chaos.)

A pitched battle took place in Rostocker Straße, where residents threw flowerpots down onto the cops' heads. A state of emergency was declared for the entire district. Even British journalists reporting on the riots were beaten up by police. Two workers were killed by the repression, and hundreds were injured. The top leaders of the union and the Social Democratic Party (SPD), however, remained completely passive — they even offered to help the authorities restore order. As a result, the strike collapsed.

Right-wing social democratic leaders like Eduard David denounced the rioters as "the dregs of society" and "the Lumpenproletariat." This is quite an astounding defamation of the SPD's own rank and file — the party had won 72% of votes in Moabit in the previous elections. One worker who was sentenced to prison was an SPD member, yet the party refused to provide him with a lawyer — he ended up taking his own life in jail. The police praised the SPD leadership for having tried to put the brakes on the movement. Solidarity only came from the party's left wing and some local organizations.

Reporters said it reminded them of 1848 in Berlin, when "troops shot down the mob before the Palace." In reality, the Moabit Unrest was more like a preview of the coming revolution in Berlin, which was less than a decade away. In both cases, "bloodthirsty amazons" — women workers — were on the front lines. The riots were also a preview of the split in the social democracy: The party rank and file wanted revolution, but the party leadership was prepared to support counterrevolutionary violence.

9.2. Butter Riots
Boxhagener Platz

Boxi is at the dead center of Friedrichshain — all the social contradictions of a neighborhood between Stalinism, squatting, and gentrification are compressed on a small patch of grass. The area was once full of squats (See Stop 7.11), but the only remnant of that time is the building at Grünberger Straße 73 with the bar Zielona Gora (now legalized). A market takes place on the square every Saturday — a tradition going back to 1905.

World War I began in summer 1914, and over the following year, the situation for working-class women in Berlin got worse and worse. Ration cards were introduced, but many products on the cards could not be found in the shops. Proletarian women spent entire days standing in lines. On the evening of October 14, 1915, women were insulted by the owners of a butter shop in Friedrichshain. In response, they smashed the windows and

took what they needed. The protests continued on the afternoon of October 16, when women and children were enraged
by high prices at the Boxhagener Platz market. Like Jesus in
the temple, they turned over the stands and expropriated the
foodstuffs.

The events at Boxi became known as the "Butter Riots" — and
they were not an isolated case. As the food situation deteriorated,
bread riots took place across the German Empire. In some cases,
these became politicized. In Neukölln, for example, a brawl at
a grocer's on Hermannstraße led, just a week later, to a protest
by 3,000 women in front of the Neukölln City Hall demanding
bread and also peace.

The first public protest against World War I was organized
by women. On March 18, 1915, which was then International
Women's Day, hundreds of socialist women gathered in front
of the Reichstag. The parliament was set to vote on yet another
round of war credits two days later, and the women were there
to support Karl Liebknecht, who had announced he would again
vote no. (See Stop 2.4) After half an hour, police broke up the
women's demonstration, but they regrouped at Brandenburg
Gate and marched to Alexanderplatz, ending at the Cemetery of
the March Fallen.

A second rally in front of the Reichstag on May 28, 1915,
brought together 1,500 women. These women were the first
workers in Germany to demonstrate against the war and the
pro-war policies of the SPD leadership — this was more than
a year before Liebknecht's May Day rally at Potsdamer Platz.
(See Stop 2.1) On March 26–28, 1915, several dozen delegates
from different countries gathered in Bern in neutral Switzerland

for the third International Socialist Women's Conference. Under the leadership of Clara Zetkin, this conference called for a "war against war." Again, this was almost half a year before the international socialist conference in Zimmerwald, Switzerland, that represented men as well.

Zetkin, the leader of the SPD's women's section, was among the most prominent anti-war activists in Germany. In the newspaper *Die Gleichheit* (Equality), she wrote that the war was being waged "for the gold and power hunger of the insensitive, unscrupulous magnates and capitalists." Her newspaper reached over 100,000 subscribers — until she was fired by the SPD leadership. Before long, women would play a central role in the revolutionary mobilizations that ended the war.

9.3. *Clara Zetkin*
Summter Straße 4, Birkenwerder

Birkenwerder is a small town in Brandenburg, just half an hour by S-Bahn from Friedrichstraße. After arriving in the village, a 10-minute walk alongside the train tracks leads to a proud white house with a red tile roof behind a fenced-in garden. This is the Birkenwerder library, and the upper floor contains a memorial to Clara Zetkin, who moved into this house in 1929. For decades, she had been a leader of the socialist women's movement in Germany and internationally. Now the elderly revolutionary needed a quiet home close to Berlin, as she had a seat in the Reichstag.

Two decades earlier, Clara Zetkin had created International Women's Day. At the second International Socialist Women's

Conference in Copenhagen in 1910, Zetkin proposed a day of struggle for working-class women. The day was originally set for March 18 to commemorate the Paris Commune of 1871, as well as the 1848 uprising in Berlin. After the Russian Revolution of 1917, Women's Day was moved to March 8 to honor the textile workers who went on strike and brought down the Tsar.

Zetkin was born in 1857 as Clara Eissner in a small town in Saxony. Despite her middle-class background, she joined the Socialist Workers Party in 1878. Not long after, the party was banned, and she fled to Paris. There she took the name of her partner, Ossip Zetkin, and had two sons, Maxim and Kostja. When Germany's Anti-Socialist Laws were lifted, Zetkin moved to Stuttgart and dedicated herself to organizing women workers. She took over as editor of the social democratic women's newspaper *Die Gleichheit* (Equality) in 1892.

During World War I, Zetkin worked closely with Rosa Luxemburg and other internationalists. She was expelled from the Social Democratic Party (SPD) along with all other opponents of the war and joined the Spartacus Group as well as the Independent Social Democratic Party (USPD). When Luxemburg split off to found a new communist party, Zetkin at first remained in the USPD, hoping to win more of its members for communism. She became a leader of the KPD in 1919, as well as the secretary of the Communist Women's International when it was founded in 1920.

On August 30, 1932, the Reichstag opened what would be its final session. In the context of a global economic crisis, the Communist Party of Germany had grown dramatically — but the

Nazi Party had grown even more: They were the largest party in the chamber with 230 seats.

At age 75, Zetkin was the Reichstag's oldest member, and thus had the right to open the session as honorary president. She had been recovering at a sanitarium in Moscow, but hurried back to Berlin for the occasion. Her voice was slow and weakened by illness, but she retained all the determination of a lifelong fighter for equality. In a 40-minute speech, she called for the working class in Germany to form a united front against the fascist threat. She closed with a revolutionary vision:

> I am opening this Congress in the fulfillment of my duties as honorary president and in the hope that despite my current infirmities, I may yet have the fortune to open as honorary president of the first Council Congress of a Soviet Germany.

After the Nazis established their dictatorship, Zetkin fled to Moscow. She died in June 1933.

A street in the middle of Berlin was named after Clara Zetkin in 1951. She likely took this ancient street herself to walk from the Friedrichstraße station to the Reichstag. Despite Zetkin's ongoing popularity among new generations of feminists, the street was renamed in 1995 — women's protests could not prevent the change to Dorotheenstraße, after the Brandenburgian princess Dorothea Sophie von Schleswig-Holstein-Sonderburg-Glücksburg. A Clara-Zetkin-Park remains in the Eastern district of Marzahn, where a statue depicts Zetkin in her long coat, just like she looked when walking arm-in-arm with Rosa Luxemburg.

9.4. Käthe Kollwitz
Kollwitzstraße 56a / Kollwitzplatz

Today, Kollwitzplatz is a symbol of gentrification — a square known for latte, brunch, and insufferably bougie babies. It is hard to imagine that in the 1990s, Prenzlauer Berg was a run-down neighborhood full of squats.

Käthe Kollwitz, originally from Königsberg in Eastern Prussia (today Kaliningrad in Russia), spent most of her life in this proletarian neighborhood. She became Germany's greatest artist of the inter-war period and was the first woman elected to the Prussian Academy of the Arts. She lived with her husband, the doctor Karl Kollwitz, at the address that is now Kollwitzstraße 56a from 1891 until the building was destroyed by a bomb in 1943. Her husband was a "poor people's doctor," and life among the working class inspired her art. Kollwitz described feeling "moved by the fate of the proletariat."

Kollwitz's work — including paintings, wood cuttings, and statues — captures the suffering and the heroism of workers. Her most famous pieces depict the uprising of the Silesian weavers in 1844 or the German Peasant Wars of the sixteenth century. After the murder of Karl Liebknecht (See Stop 3.11), Kollwitz made a print *In Memoriam of Karl Liebknecht*. The workers mourning over the corpse of the communist leader look like the apostles grieving for Jesus. Liebknecht himself had never shied away from biblical motifs, writing in his final article that the "Road to Golgotha of the German working class is not yet completed — but the Day of Redemption is near."

Kollwitz was never a member of the SPD, the KPD, or any other party, but she was sympathetic to the ideas of socialism and communism. In 1932, the artist signed a call — alongside Albert Einstein, Heinrich Mann, and others — for the workers' parties and trade unions to form a single left slate for the elections.

She passed away in 1945, just days before the war ended, and was buried at the Central Cemetery of Friedrichsfelde, also known as the Socialists' Cemetery. (See Stop 3.13) A Kollwitz-Museum at Fasanenstraße 24 in Charlottenburg opened in 1986. The square was dedicated to her in 1950, and a statue was added in 1961. In the years after the wall came down, Kollwitzplatz was not known for yuppies. Quite the opposite: While the Revolutionary May Day demonstrations usually took place in Kreuzberg (See Stops 6.5 to 6.7), in the 1990s they made it as far north as Prenzlauer Berg. On May 1, 1996, for example, barricades were erected on Kollwitzplatz to block police water cannons.

Today, Kollwitz's most prominent work is located at the Neue Wache (New Guard) on Unter den Linden. The building was once a guard house for the palace across the road. In 1957, the German Democratic Republic converted it into a Memorial to the Victims of Fascism and Militarism. This included the remains of an unknown soldier and an unknown prisoner of a concentration camp, with an eternal flame burning next to a large glass prism.

The building was redone again in 1993, now as the Federal Republic's Memorial to the Victims of War and Tyranny. The shift in name has an ideological function: Fascism is no longer singled out, as the new regime attempts to put an equal sign between Nazism and Stalinism, supposedly the "two German dictatorships." Ironically, the new centerpiece of the memorial is an enlarged copy of the statue *Mother with Her Dead Son* — sculpted by an artist who supported and was supported by communists. Kollwitz's son Peter had died on the battlefield in October 1914, after she had supported his decision to enlist while still a minor.

9.5. Paragraph 218
former Sportpalast — Potsdamer Straße 172

When it opened in 1910, the Berlin Sport Palace was the city's biggest arena. Up to 14,000 people could squeeze inside to see ice skating, hockey, or boxing matches with Max Schmeling. Political rallies were also held here: Social democrats, communists, and Nazis all used the cavernous space. The most famous event took place in early 1943: Two weeks after the German defeat at Stalingrad, the Nazi propaganda minister Joseph Goebbels gave his infamous speech declaring "total war."

Less well-known: The Sportpalast was also the site of the largest rally for abortion rights in Weimar Germany.

Paragraph 218 of the German criminal code of 1871 prohibited terminating a pregnancy, with punishments of up to five years of hard labor. Socialist women, as well as bourgeois feminists, protested against this law with the slogan "your tummy belongs to you." In the 1920s, communists called for the abolition of Paragraph 218, while social democrats at least wanted to modify it to allow the procedure in the first trimester.

Yet the 1920s saw only minor improvements: A reform in 1926 reduced sentences from forced labor to normal prison, while a court ruled that women could get an abortion if their lives were in danger. During the Weimar years, 60,000 women were convicted under Paragraph 218. Doctors estimated that every year, up to 10,000 women died as a result of clandestine abortions.

"What good is women's right to vote" asked Else Kienle, a doctor and activist from Stuttgart, "if they have to remain machines for giving birth, without their own free will?" Kienle was arrested in early 1931 along with the doctor Friedrich Wolf. Both were charged with providing abortions for commercial gain.

Wolf had been a member of the Communist Party since 1928. The following year, he wrote a play titled *Cyankali* about a working-class couple confronted with a pregnancy they couldn't afford. The title refers to potassium cyanide, a popular means for ending a pregnancy on the sly. The play was performed across Germany and was made into a film in 1930.*

A Committee of Struggle Against Paragraph 218 organized rallies in different cities demanding freedom for Kienle and Wolf. Wolf, well-known for his play and supported by a mass party, was released on bail. Kienle, however, had to go on a hunger strike. After seven days, she lost consciousness and was let out of prison.

One month later, Kienle was the keynote speaker at a rally against Paragraph 218 at Berlin's Sportpalast. On April 15, 1931, up to 15,000 people heard her declare: "As we know that every criminal law can only result in additional misery, we call for entirely new rules with no penalties of any kind." A police spy noted with alarm that the attendees included many elegantly dressed women and girls.

Later, Kienle and Wolf both travelled to the Soviet Union to see how the procedure was offered for free without any legal

* Wolf's son Markus later became East Germany's top spy. (See Stops 7.7 and 7.9)

restrictions. (In 1936, however, Stalin had abortion re-criminal-ized.) Kienle continued performing abortions and published a book: *Women — From the Diary of a Woman Doctor*. Persecuted by German courts and harassed by Nazis, Kienle fled the country in late 1932, and eventually made it to New York City, where she died in 1970.

The Nazis made Paragraph 218 more repressive — by 1943, the law called for the death penalty for providing abortions for commercial gain. At the same time, the fascists sterilized and murdered people they considered inferior on the basis of their racist and eugenicist ideology. Opponents of abortion are never, on close examination, "pro-life."

Paragraph 218 is still on the books in Germany. (See Stop 9.11) Bertolt Brecht's Ballad to Paragraph 218, in which a doctor patronizes a woman who wants to end a pregnancy, is thus still relevant today:

You see, our state needs people / To operate our machines. / You'll make a simply splendid little mummy / Producing factory fodder from your tummy / That's what your body's for, / and you know it, what's more / And it's laid down by law / And now get this straight: / You'll soon be a mother, just wait.

The Sport Palace was bombed during the war. It reopened in 1953, but was torn down 20 years later. The arena was replaced by a massive public housing complex called the Pallaseum: a 12-story building stretching over the Pallasstraße and an old Nazi bunker. People refer to it as the Social Palace.

9.6. Women's Center
Hornstraße 2

The turrets and balconies of this majestic white apartment building are typical of the Gründerzeit. Today, this is the extremely nice part of Kreuzberg — even more so since the abandoned train tracks at the end of the street were converted into the post-industrial Gleisdreieckspark. It's hard to imagine how run down this neighborhood was 50 years ago, when just about anyone could move into a palatial yet decrepit apartment.

Here, in the storefront on the ground floor, is where Berlin's first women's center opened its doors in early 1973. The founders included Helke Sander, who had been in the Action Committee for Women's Liberation (See Stop 5.8), the lesbian group of the Homosexual Action West Berlin (See Stop 8.6) and the women's group Brot und Rosen, which had taken its name from the Bread and Roses strike by textile workers in Lawrence, Massachusetts in 1912.

No men were allowed. Small, autonomous groups of women engaged in consciousness raising (sharing experiences as women under patriarchy), political activities, and medical counseling. The Women's Center was run by radical feminists — socialist and communist women, in contrast, preferred to organize alongside men in revolutionary organizations of different stripes.

Germany's second-wave feminist movement took up the struggle against Paragraph 218, which had been interrupted 40 years earlier. The Women's Center did not just organize protests to demand the right to abortion, but also offered consultations about pregnancy and contraception. On June 6, 1971, the cover of *Stern* magazine pictured 374 women who had signed a declaration: "We've had abortions!" The next step came three years later: Fourteen doctors announced that they were going to conduct an abortion in public. Up to 3,000 illegal abortions were taking place every day in West Germany, and they were determined to end the hypocrisy.

This procedure was carried out inside the Women's Center on March 9, 1974, and cameras from the public TV news program *Panorama* were rolling. The footage was set to air two days later. Just an hour before airtime, however, management cancelled the segment. The Catholic Church had filed charges. In protest, the editors of *Panorama* broadcast a live shot of their empty studio for 45 minutes. In the following days, women occupied different public TV stations demanding the show be emitted.

The Women's Center moved to Stresemannstraße 40 in 1977, where it remained for several years. Alice Schwarzer, a leader of the protests against Paragraph 218 in the early 1970s, is now among Germany's most conservative feminists: a ferocious opponent of sex workers, trans women, and immigrants, and a friend to cops.

9.7. Immigrant Women's Squat
Kottbusser Straße 8

Kottbusser Damm / Kottbusser Straße is the artery connecting Kreuzberg and Neukölln, the two rapidly changing immigrant neighborhoods where Berlin's pulsing contradictions are at their sharpest. The elegant tan building at Kottbusser Straße 8, with its almost royal balcony, is now home to a bicycle shop — a cooperative in which the workers run things collectively.

The area around Kottbusser Tor was once the center of the West Berlin squatting scene. (See Stop 6.1) When we picture squatters, we most likely see young men with dyed hair and leather jackets. But this is not the whole story.

Kottbusser Straße 8 was occupied by eight Turkish and Kurdish women and their children in February 1981. They were taking a literacy class at the migrants' association TIO (Meeting and Information Place for Migrants, which still exists today at Reuterstraße 78 in Neukölln) and they began to talk about what so many people in the neighborhood were doing: occupying buildings. As single immigrant women, they faced terrible racism on the housing market. They decided to act the very next day.

As soon as the women and children entered the building, which stood empty awaiting renovations, they were attacked by construction workers. They managed to barricade themselves inside one of the apartments. Demonstrators gathered on the street to express solidarity, and soon the communal housing company GSW agreed to hand over the keys.

The new squat was started by immigrant women, but soon joined by German leftists, and it was hard to establish a common culture. The former spent long days with factory work and childcare, while the latter dedicated themselves to demonstrations and plenaries. The project eventually fell apart. The GSW was privatized by the SPD and DIE LINKE in 2005, and its apartments now belong to the private company Deutsche Wohnen.

Thirty years later, immigrant women created a new squat in Kreuzberg. When refugees took over the former Gerhart-Hauptmann-Schule in late 2012, one floor of the building was turned into an International Women's Space. (See Stop 6.10) After the eviction of the school, the IWS continued the work to "form a women's front within the Refugee Movement that brings the fights against both racism and sexism together." In just about any struggle in Berlin, women have been on the front lines — though they do not always make it into the history books. (See Stops 2.6 and 6.9)

9.8. *Audre Lorde*
Audre-Lorde-Straße — former Manteuffelstraße

Audre Lorde, born in 1934 in Harlem, described herself thus: "black, lesbian, feminist, mother, poet, warrior."

In 1984, Lorde was a guest professor at the John F. Kennedy Institute for North American Studies at the Free University of Berlin. That institute sits on a street with a colonial name: Lansstraße in Dahlem. (See Stop 1.13) She returned to the city again and again, with her Berlin Years lasting until her death in 1992.

Lorde did not just dedicate herself to intellectual work: She was an activist who spent time at the women's center Schokofabrik at Mariannenstraße 6 in Kreuzberg. The former chocolate factory, which was abandoned and falling apart, was occupied by women in 1981 — it remains open to this day. Lorde found it heartwarming to see women creating a space for themselves out of the rubble.

She helped Afro-Germans get organized — Lorde supported the publication of May Ayim's work, for example. (See Next Stop) Lorde's time in the city had a lasting effect on Berlin leftists, who gained understanding of the intersections between racism, sexism, and queerphobia. Anticipating reflections by activists today, Lorde emphasized that self-care "is not self-indulgence. It is self-preservation, and that is an act of political warfare." For a detailed map of Lorde's time in Berlin, see: www.audrelordeberlin.com

In early 2019, the district council of Friedrichshain-Kreuzberg voted that a street would be named after Audre Lorde. This had originally been one of the proposals for renaming M-Straße. (See Stop 1.5) Two years later, they voted that the northern half of Manteuffelstraße (between Skalitzer Straße and Köpenicker Straße) should be called Audre-Lorde-Straße. The southern half will continue to honor Otto Theodor von Manteuffel, the prime minister of Prussia who helped reverse democratic reforms in the decade after the failed revolution of 1848. What an intersection of street names! Kreuzberg has plenty of roads named after Prussian reactionaries — changing them all will be no small undertaking. (See Stop 3.9)

9.9. May Ayim
May-Ayim-Ufer

> "i will be african
> even if you want me to be german
> and i will be german
> even if my blackness does not suit you"

This short cobblestone street runs along the Spree river. This is where the Oberbaum Bridge with its fantastical red-brick towers connects Kreuzberg in the West and Friedrichshain in the East. This bridge once marked the border between the two halves of the city. A plaque on the water's edge commemorates the five people who drowned here while trying to escape East Germany — as well as five children from the West who died while playing in the water. The memorial leaves a bitter aftertaste when we recall that Germany has no monument for the nameless thousands of people who drown every year just outside the walls of Fortress Europe.

The street was named Groebenufer in 1895, after the Brandenburgian aristocrat Friedrich Otto von der Groeben who had established the first German colony in 1683. (See Stop 1.1) The christening took place at the zenith of German colonialism, just one year before the Colonial Exhibition in Treptower Park. (See Stop 1.8)

This was the first colonial street name in Berlin to be changed. In 2010, it was dedicated to the Afro-German poet and activist May Ayim, whose work showed how the legacies of colonialism shape German society today.

May Ayim was raised as Sylvia Opitz in Hamburg in 1960. She was adopted as a baby and grew up as a Black child in a white family. She was always made to feel different — over time, she realized that her experience was not unique. Afro-Germans had been around for centuries, yet they are almost entirely ignored by mainstream society, and treated as if they are about to emigrate any second.

Her thesis on the social and cultural history of Afro-Germans was later published in an anthology in German and English, with the support of Audre Lorde: *Showing Our Colors: Afro-German Women Speak Out*. May Ayim was one of the founders of the Initiative of Black People in Germany (ISD). Traveling to Ghana to meet her biological father in 1992, she gave up the name of her adoptive family and took that of her Ghanaian relatives, going from May Opitz to May Ayim.

Having struggled with suicidal impulses since childhood, May Ayim suffered a collapse in summer 1996. She ended her life on August 9 by jumping from the 14th floor of a building in Kreuzberg.

9.10. Angela Davis
Friedrichstadt-Palast — Friedrichstraße 107

The largest theater in Berlin has all the hallmarks of East German modernism: stained glass, brass trim, and lots of concrete. Today it hosts musical reviews and the Berlinale film festival. For decades, the Friedrichstadt-Palast was a center of GDR pop culture — but not in its current location.

The original theater was across the road. It opened in 1868 as a market hall, before being rebuilt as a circus and then as a theater. That is why the small street is still called "Am Zirkus." The name Friedrichstadt-Palast was bestowed by the Soviets in 1947, and the Free German Youth (FDJ) held its founding congress there. The original theater had to be torn down in 1980, and its replacement on Friedrichstraße was completed in 1984. Since 2014, a building called "yoo" with a hotel and condominiums — including Berlin's most expensive apartment — stands on the site of the ancient theater. Because history loves irony, this is all behind the statue of Bertolt Brecht.

On September 11, 1972, a member of the Black Panther Party and the Communist Party of the USA spoke at the Friedrichstadt-Palast. With a large Afro and an even bigger smile, Angela Davis was East Germany's biggest pop star. While she had been in prison in New York and California awaiting trial on trumped-up murder charges, East Germans had sent her one million postcards in solidarity ("one million roses for Angela").

When Davis arrived in East Berlin, she was bigger than the Beatles (not to mention Jesus, who didn't get much shrift in an increasingly atheistic country). A crowd of 50,000 young people cheered as she got out of the airplane at Schönefeld airport. "We welcome Angela to the finally liberated land of Marx and Engels," an FDJ leader called out. State security, accustomed to being in perfect control of public life, later admitted that they had been overwhelmed by the excited crowds.

On stage that evening, wearing the blue uniform shirt of the FDJ, Davis denounced American racism and imperialism. Her speech, titled "Not Only My Victory," recognized the support she had received from the GDR and other socialist countries. The same day, she met with SED leader Eric Honecker who praised her "struggle in the citadel of world imperialism."

Davis also visited the Berlin Wall, laying flowers at a memorial for Reinhold Huhn at the corner of Jerusalemer Straße and Schützenstraße. Huhn was an East German border soldier who was shot and killed by a man who was smuggling people across the border in 1962. Davis promised that "When we return to the USA, we shall undertake to tell our people the truth about the true function of this border." Fidel Castro had been there a few years previous.

Davis returned to East Berlin in 1973 for the World Festival of Youth and Students. At this international celebration, East German authorities allowed unprecedented freedoms, and to some it felt like "Red Woodstock" — though there were limits.

SED boss Eric Honecker meets Angela Davis in East Berlin on September 11, 1972. See Stop 9.10. Bundesarchiv, Bild 183-L0911-029 / Koard, Peter / CC-BY-SA 3.0.

(See Stop 8.10) Davis eventually earned a PhD in philosophy from East Berlin's Humboldt University.

East Germany offered refuge to persecuted leftists from different parts of the world. Michelle Bachelet, the future president of Chile, fled her country after she was arrested and tortured by the military dictatorship. Bachelet was able to study medicine in the GDR, as one of at least 2,000 Chilean refugees. But at the same time, the Stalinist state was not free of racism, and the treatment of "contract workers" from Vietnam and other "socialist brother countries" was particularly brutal.

9.11. Palace of the Republic
former Palast der Republik — Humboldt Forum
— Schlossplatz

Berlin's re-built City Palace is officially called the Humboldt Forum. (See Stop 2.2) The Prussian nostalgists behind the project were hoping to have their cake and eat it too: They recreated this monument to Prussia's authoritarian, militaristic, and colonial traditions. But by naming it after the brothers Wilhelm and Alexander von Humboldt, they hoped it would gain a whiff of enlightenment. The result is a terrible mishmash, in both form and content. Only part of the facade is in the old baroque style, while much of the inside looks like an austere shopping mall. The exhibitions are no less contradictory: Looted colonial art from the collections of the Ethnological Museum is just one floor away from a radical Berlin history of punks, trans activists, and revolutionaries.

The original palace was heavily damaged in World War II, and the German Democratic Republic (GDR) cleared away the ruins in 1950. Why were German elites in the twenty-first century so eager to rebuild a drab palace without so much as a king to live inside? Because this was the site of the Palace of the Republic, the East German parliament building which opened its doors in 1976. Its bronze-tinted windows mirrored downtown East Berlin for the next three decades. With thousands of ultramodern light fixtures illuminating the white marble foyer, people referred to it as Erich's lamp shop (in reference to SED boss Erich Honecker). At the end of the nineteenth century, the workers' movement had built People's Houses; inspired by this model, the Palace contained enormous meeting halls (including one for the GDR's People's Chamber), restaurants, galleries, and spaces for music. Santana, Harry Belafonte, and Mercedes Sosa all performed here.

The official reason for demolishing the building was that it was full of asbestos. Yet West Berlin's International Congress Centrum, of less architectural interest or historic significance, is also full of asbestos, and it will be refurbished. The Palace of the Republic had to be obliterated because it was physical proof that German imperialism had once lost control of half of its capital. The demolition began in 2006, exactly 30 years after the Palace opened.

After the wall came down, East Germany elected a new People's Chamber in March 1990. (See Stop 7.10) Its only task was to facilitate annexation by the Federal Republic of Germany. This did not just mean privatizing the state-run economy — it also meant applying all of West Germany's laws, including the ban on abortion. (See Stop 9.5)

After 1945, Paragraph 218 remained in force in both halves of Germany, meaning that abortion and contraception were prohibited. East Germany started to allow abortions for medical reasons in 1950. West Germany, in contrast, needed until 1953 just to remove the death penalty from the law. (Even though the death penalty had been abolished with the constitution 1949.)

A new mass movement for abortion rights emerged in West Germany in the late 1960s. (See Stop 9.6) Ironically, these protests were only successful on the other side of the wall: The GDR's People's Chamber voted to legalize abortion in 1972, allowing the procedure in the first trimester without any restrictions or obligatory consultations. The East German CDU voted against the reform — the only case of dissent in the 40-year history of the GDR's parliament.

In the West, things moved much more slowly. In 1974, the social democratic government tried to legalize abortion in the first trimester, but the conservative opposition sued, and the constitutional court nixed the law. In 1976, a reform left the ban in place — but a new Paragraph 218a decriminalized abortion under certain conditions.

German reunification meant that abortion would be recriminalized in the former GDR. On April 22, 1990 — half a year before East Germany was swallowed up — 1,000 people gathered at the Lustgarten (Pleasure Garden) opposite the Palace of the Republic. They brought a petition with 17,000 signatures to the GDR's still-functioning parliament. One much-photographed banner read: "If the condom has a hole, dear Lothar, what then?" (referring to conservative politician Lothar de Maizière, the GDR's final prime minister). Further demonstrations took place across East and even West Germany on June 16. Yet conservative politicians, supported by the state-funded churches, insisted that women would be irresponsible with their reproductive capabilities if the state did not control them.

Reproductive rights in reunified Germany were contradictory until 1995, when a new law went into effect. To this day, Paragraph 218 still reads: "Whoever terminates a pregnancy incurs a penalty of imprisonment for a term not exceeding three years or a fine." The following paragraph lists the conditions under which this punishment is not applied.

Thus, well into the twenty-first century, abortion remains illegal in Germany. As a result, it is not covered by insurance, nor taught in medical schools. Women need to pass through an obligatory consultation — which in many places is only offered by church-run institutions — and a three-day waiting period before they can interrupt a pregnancy. Doctors have been fined thousands of euros for "advertising abortion," which means nothing more than mentioning that they offer the procedure on their websites. Every year in September, several thousand Christian fundamentalists hold a so-called "March for Life" through Berlin. And every year, thousands of feminists and leftists block this parade of reaction.

10

Afterword:
Where This Book Was Written

As I was writing this book in mid-2021, the city was under partial lockdown. Most days I took my bike to one of two spots. Each one is a green refuge created by the chaotic history described in this volume. They provided the peace necessary to write. "Here, I am a person," as Goethe put it, "here, I dare to be." It wouldn't feel right to end a guidebook without mentioning them.

10.1. Tempelhofer Feld
S-Bhf Tempelhof

This must be the weirdest park in Europe: Right in the middle of the city, Berlin has an enormous field, more than two kilometers across, that is completely empty. There are not even many trees — just endless expanses of grass broken up by asphalt streams. Look closer, however, and Tempelhofer Feld is full of tiny urban ecosystems. There are protected areas for nesting birds, sprawling community gardens, and even a baseball diamond (a rare site in Germany).

This was once a parade ground for the Prussian military. On May 1, 1933, Adolf Hitler held a massive rally here for the "Day of National Labor" in an attempt to co-opt the workers' May Day traditions. In 1936, the Nazis built Tempelhof Airport in their gargantuan style, with a hall that stretches 1.2 kilometers. Rumors about seven levels of cavernous basements below the field are, unfortunately, untrue — or at the very least, I have not been able to find the entrance. This was also the site of the Columbia Concentration Camp that opened in 1934 — a memorial is just north of the field at the corner of Columbiadamm and Züllichauer Straße.

The United States military took over the airport after the war, and this is where most of the planes landed during the Berlin Airlift in 1948. Tempelhof lost its status as West Berlin's main airport around 1968, with Tegel's iconic hexagonal terminal opening in 1974. But Tempelhof remained a commercial airport where large propeller planes could land right in the middle of the city. It finally closed in 2008.

The now-empty field nonetheless remained sealed off with barbed wire. Attempts to "squat an airport" in 2009 were beaten back by 1,800 police with water cannons. But this created political pressure, and a park was opened in 2010 — a much-needed lung for the overcrowded working-class district of Neukölln. (See Stop 4.1) City planners intended for this space to be only temporary — soon, luxury condos would be built around a reduced and manicured park in the center. But in 2011, the initiative 100% Tempelhofer Feld was launched to keep the space empty.

Berlin's government made all kinds of promises: They would sprinkle a few units of affordable housing amongst the properties for speculators, and maybe even a library. They held pathetically stage-managed "public forums" to sell their plans. But a referendum was held in 2014, and 64.3% of voters wanted to ban all construction. There were not only huge majorities in Neukölln and Kreuzberg, as had been expected, but in every single Berlin district.

Today, millions of people visit Tempelhofer Feld every year, for everything from drinking to kiteboarding to writing anti-capitalist guidebooks. The successful referendum showed that mass campaigns can keep public space out of the hands of capital. This was a direct inspiration for the campaign to expropriate the city's biggest landlords that began collecting signatures in 2020. That initiative gathered 330,000 signatures in just four months — and the number one spot to find supporters was this enormous field.

10.2. Animal Park
Tierpark — Am Tierpark 125

Berlin has one world-class zoo that provided the name for the central train station in the west: Bahnhof Zoologischer Garten. Germany's oldest zoo opened in 1844, and today it attracts visitors from all over the world. But the city has a second world-class zoo in Friedrichsfelde that isn't full of tourists. Most people who visit the Tierpark (Animal Park) are from East Berlin, as if the wall were still standing

After the division of the city, East Berlin needed its own zoo so that families wouldn't travel to the West to see exotic animals. Zoologist Heinrich Dathe was originally skeptical, given that there were already several well-established zoos across the German Democratic Republic. But once he saw the palace gardens in Friedrichsfelde, which had been seized from the House of Treskow during the Soviet land reform, Dathe quickly took over the project.

The Tierpark was opened in 1955 by GDR president Wilhelm Pieck, who had once been arrested alongside Rosa Luxemburg. (See Stop 7.1) The Friedrichsfelde Palace had stood abandoned after the war and was preserved for several years by Charlotte von Mahlsdorf. (See Stop 8.9) Before more permanent structures could be set up, the palace was used to house chimpanzees.

Given the GDR's chronic shortages of metal, the Tierpark relied on creative recycling: The polar bear enclosure, for example, was built out of the ruins of the former Reichsbank. Lacking resources for metal bars, gibbons and lemurs were placed on islands surrounded by moats. Those enclosures still stand today.

Over the decades, the Tierpark built some of the world's most modern animal houses, including the Alfred-Brehm-Haus for large cats (finished in 1963) and the Pachyderm House (opened in 1989). Dathe hosted a weekly show on East German TV about animals, becoming a kind of East German Johnny Carson.

The Tierpark struggled to survive in the reunified city. It was merged with its Western competitor and needed subsidies of several million euros a year. Today, the West gets the top-shelf animals like pandas, but the East includes walk-in enclosures for ruffed lemurs and kangaroos — it actually has more species of mammals.

Above all, the Tierpark shows what is possible with expropriation. The Western Zoo was donated by the King of Prussia, and it has to squeeze onto just 35 hectares. The Eastern Zoo was confiscated from aristocrats, and it has 4.5 times as much space. It is the largest zoo in Europe, and incredibly serene — peaceful enough to write a book.

GDR president Wilhelm Pieck (wearing a hat in the middle) opens the Tierpark in East Berlin on July 2, 1955. Next to him is Tierpark director Heinrich Dathe. In the background is Friedrichsfelde Palace. See Stop 10.2. Bundesarchiv, Bild 183-31492-0001 / CC-BY-SA 3.0.

About the Author

Why would you want to get your Berlin history from a dude from the United States? Well, as Kurt Tucholsky put it in the 1920s, "the real Berliner comes from Breslau." (Breslau is today the Polish city of Wrocław.) It's actually pretty rare to meet someone who was born and raised in Berlin. It is the *Zugezogene*, the people who moved here, who are angriest about how the city is going to the dogs. Today, a century after Tucholsky, the real Berliner probably comes from Bochum, Budapest, or Baghdad. What holds us all together is our profound dislike for this place — though apparently, we hate it just a little bit less than everywhere else. We love it because we can complain about it together.

For me, this story starts on a May Day in the early 2000s. The long night around Kottbusser Tor in Kreuzberg used to be a festival of destructive joy: Cars were flipped over and set alight, cobblestones flew overhead toward the bulky green cop uniforms, and mobs of people pushed back and forth like tides. Although I am not much of a street fighter myself, I was enthralled.

After several years of demonstrating and helping out with the organizing, I began showing friends around: "This is where the first Revolutionary May Day demonstration started." Or: "This is where that supermarket was burned down in 1987." Those friends loved it and sent along their friends. Before long, I was taking total strangers down a standardized route. That's how I became a tour guide.

Since I started giving tours, I have learned that I am on the autism spectrum. It makes perfect sense: I am not great at social

271

cues, eye contact, or small talk. But I am very good at getting slightly obsessed with a topic and speaking about it for two hours straight. This is not good at a party, but very good for a walking tour. In fact, these tours are my autism superpower.

If you would like to reach the author, perhaps for a guided tour in Berlin, check out:

revolutionaryberlin@gmail.com
revolutionaryberlin.wordpress.com
facebook.com/revolutionaryberlin
instagram.com/revolutionaryberlin

Index

Thanks to our Patreon subscriber:

Ciaran Kane

Who has shown generosity and comradeship in support of our publishing.

Check out the other perks you get by subscribing to our Patreon – visit patreon.com/plutopress.

Subscriptions start from £3 a month.